THROUGH CHARLIE'S EYES

The Remarkable Story of
A YOUNG MAN FACING THE BATTLE OF A LIFETIME

THROUGH, CHARLIE'S EYES

The remarkable story of
A YOUNG MAN FACING THE BATTLE OF A LIFETIME

by
LAKEN LOVELY
CHARLIE LOVELY

AMBASSADOR INTERNATIONAL
GREENVILLE, SOUTH CAROLINA & BELFAST, NORTHERN IRELAND

www.ambassador-international.com

THROUGH CHARLIE'S EYES
The Remarkable Story of a Young Man Facing the Battle of a Lifetime

Printed in the United States of America
ISBN 978-1-935507-06-2

Cover Design & Page Layout by David Siglin of A&E Media

AMBASSADOR INTERNATIONAL
Emerald House
427 Wade Hampton Blvd.
Greenville, SC 29609, USA
www.ambassador-international.com

AMBASSADOR PUBLICATIONS
Providence House
Ardenlee Street
Belfast, BT6 8QJ, Northern Ireland, UK
www.ambassador-productions.com

The colophon is a trademark of Ambassador

Some names of hosptial staff and patients have been changed.

Dedication

For every believer and every person who's ever witnessed a miracle, or longed for one.

"I can do all things through Christ which strengthens me."
Philippians 4:13

Table of Contents

Acknowledgements

First and foremost, I would like to thank my Lord and Savior for giving me faith, hope, and love. Of course, I thank my little brother, Charlie, for being an inspiration to me and everyone he touches and for bestowing upon me the honor of telling his story and carrying on his legacy. I wouldn't be the person I am today if it wasn't for him. He is my angel and this is all for him.

My family is my everything and as my fellow wounded soldiers, they have helped carry me through this journey and honor God and Charlie in all that I accomplish. My father, Tim Lovely and my mother, Lorna Lovely are the strongest people I know, thank you both for giving me my brothers and my life and thank you for not giving up and being our guides as we figured out how to walk with out our sunshine. My older brother, Blake, and my youngest brother, Chandler, how could I ever say thank you enough for my brothers, you're my people! Chandler, you are a gift from God, and I thank Charlie everyday for praying for you and bringing you to us. Your smile is the beacon of light that promises me there is a forever. Blake, no one else will ever know how I truly feel, except for you. Thank you for teaching me how to be an awesome older sister and a pseudo-mother for our two little brothers, you encouraged me in all my pursuits. To my whole family, for giving me the ability to take this project where it is today.

I would like to thank the one man that Charlie gave his blessings to for me, Chris Hurst, for being my rock, my shoulder to cry on, and my coach at the times that I thought I couldn't go any further.

I would like to thank Edie Hand for being a mentor for me, not only as a writer, but as a grieving big sister. I do believe that Charlie brought me to you, and I feel so blessed to have met some one with such a caring, giving heart. Thank you for helping me go so far.

Thank you to my college professor and mentor, Dr. Susan Thompson, for believing in me and encouraging me in my writing pursuits. You always encouraged me to be my best and I'm very blessed to be able to call you a friend.

I would also like to thank every member of our large and extraordinarily close family, every one of you played a magnificent role in the story of Charlie's Life.

Also, thank you, the reader of this book, for taking an interest in Charlie's story.

Introduction

When I was twenty-two years old, I watched as my hero, my kindred spirit, my confidant, my protector, and my best friend slipped away from this world and into the next. I stood beside my little brother and held his hand, as I listened to the ventilator in his small hospital room pump air into his weak lungs. We had come to the end of an unexpected, short, roller coaster ride with cancer. After only sixty-two days of therapy including two ICU stays, numerous pokes and prods including regular spinal taps, and one life-threatening surgery, the Great Physician was ready to take the strong spirit that lie within the beautiful body of my littler brother, Charlie, that had so unexpectedly and so tragically become overcome with a sickness so powerful his earthly body could no longer fight it.

When Charlie was first diagnosed with the cancer that would take his life, he confided in me that he wanted to write a memoir on his experience with childhood cancer in hopes of shedding light on this struggle that all too many families must endure. I made a promise to him that if, for whatever the reason, he could not complete his memoir, I would do it for him. On the day of Charlie's funeral, I pulled the small composition notebook he had left for me, with his scribbled handwriting inside, out of his book bag that he had carried with him every day. Charlie and I were only six years apart in age, and as the middle children of our family, we had developed a special bond. We were a team on this earth, and I believe that our partnership carries on. I want to make it very clear that I did not write this memoir alone.

Although my teammate no longer walks in his physical body on earth, I believe that we carry on our partnership, he in the spiritual world, and I here, on earth.

I hope that the message of this novel will change the lives of all those who take the time to sit and read it. Life is what you make it, and I had the privilege of learning that through a true gift in my life, my little brother with an old soul.

Charlie spent his entire life smiling and laughing. No matter what situation he was put in during his short lifetime, he always made the best of it. At times when other people would have lain down and given up, Charlie stood up and shined his bright light on everyone else and laughed and joked. It didn't matter how serious the situation, Charlie could make a joke of it and make everyone laugh. He knew how to find the humor in everything in life, and he always wanted to share it with everyone around him.

———————————

I remember the day Charlie first came home, less than twenty-four hours after he was born, on Halloween evening. The little baby with bright red, round cheeks beamed a light all over our home. He literally never stopped laughing and smiling. The first time I met him, just minutes after he came into this world, he smiled at me and sixteen years and two months later, a few seconds before he fell asleep for the last time, he smiled at me. As I sat there with him, I remembered when I was six years old, and my mom was about half way through her pregnancy with Charlie. I quietly opened the door to my mom and dad's bedroom and saw them crying together. They didn't notice me as I stood there with the door slightly cracked, staring in. I silently closed the door back and went to my room and cried. I knew that they were crying because the little brother that was in my mom's belly wasn't there anymore, I had overheard them talking. I prayed that somehow, God would make it not true, and I could still have a little brother. The next day, when my mother went to her final visit with the doctor that had helped her through her pregnancy with Charlie, the doctor decided to try and do one last sonogram, just to be sure the baby was gone. I watched him squirt gel on my mom's belly and as he moved that small plastic wand around her stretched skin, he caught something, a strong little heartbeat. He was still there! This time we all cried again, but this time we cried tears of joy. About five months later, we greeted the person that became the sunshine of our family.

As I sat there watching my little brother sleep with the machines around him keeping him alive, I prayed that God would make this cancer and everything that came with it untrue too. I prayed that he would give us another miracle, and save Charlie just one more time. Even though I felt that my prayers were not heard, I was given peace and I believe I got to see a miracle that New Year's Eve that Charlie left this world. I hope that through the pages of this book, as you follow Charlie's journey, you will too see the true miracle behind Charlie's life as you witness it through his eyes.

Tab, Mom, Chan, and I in Nashville, Tn.

New School

The bell rang acknowledging the start of a new school day, and the start of my new life. I looked over my schedule, preparing myself for the rest of the day: English, Gym, History, Parenting, Geometry, Chemistry, and most importantly, basketball practice.

I was nervous that morning before school, but I was confident that my first day would be a success. I was still a little anxious to see what this new school had in store for me. Sitting in a small metal desk in my homeroom class, I looked around at all of the unfamiliar faces. I couldn't remember ever being in a situation like this before, where I honestly didn't know anyone in the room. I'd have to make some new friends. I turned to the girl beside me and tried to strike up a conversation.

"I'm Charlie."

"I know," she said, "Most people here know who you are. You transferred from Walker to play basketball here."

I was a little surprised to hear that word of my transfer had spread to people I had never even met before.

"You were a pretty big deal at Walker," the girl continued, "Why would you want to come here?"

A little flattered I just said, "Basketball…I can be a big deal here too right?"

She laughed. I was glad she got my joke.

"What's your name?" I asked.

"Tiffany."

"Nice to meet you." I gave her a smile and turned back around. Most people couldn't understand the passion that I had for basketball. Many of my friends had questioned my decision to transfer to our rival high school just for basketball. After all, I would be leaving behind the friends I grew up with and my position as class president and class favorite for the uncertainty of a new school full of strangers. However, I wanted to have a successful career in basketball and I had to take a chance to make myself as great as possible. That's how I ended up at a brand new school in my sophomore year in high school.

After the announcements and our moment of silence the bell rang again signaling that it was time for my first class. I decided to stop by my locker first, mostly because I had time, and because I wanted to see where it was and whom I would be next to for the rest of the year. I walked the halls looking for locker 507. Scanning, I turned left 600, 550, 525, 505, 507! I found my locker at the end of a hallway near two double doors that lead outside. There was a large vent hanging from the ceiling and making a lot of noise. Other kids were all around me; one grabbed my arm, "Charlie!"

I turned, relieved to see one of my teammates who was a senior. "How's the first day going?"

"Pretty good so far."

"Well, we're just getting started. I'm sure I don't have any classes with you, but I'll see you at practice."

I giggled at him, "Alright."

The day passed by quickly and before I knew it I was walking to the cafeteria for lunch period. I hadn't even thought about where I would sit or whom I would sit with until I walked into the crowded lunchroom and stepped into a line of other hungry and rowdy teenagers. I scanned faces in the sea of kids, hoping to see someone I recognized as I waited in line. I was about to give up when I felt a tap on my shoulder; the teammate I had seen earlier in the day was in line behind me.

We went through the line together as he filled me in on the inside workings of the school, where the basketball players sat, where the cheerleaders sat, and so on. I got pizza and my friend piled a load of fries onto his plate and then covered them with ranch dressing. I tried it later on in the year, and it was actually really good. I followed him to a table on the side of the cafeteria furthest from where the teachers and administrators were. We kept those seats for the rest of the time I attended school there.

After more classes, the bell rang for the last period of the day, basketball practice. I had been looking forward to practice all day. I worked on my game all summer and I was eager to get on the court and scrimmage with teammates. Getting dressed out before practice put me at ease. I knew the other guys on the team pretty well, so that wasn't an issue, but mainly getting prepared to go out and play my best really held my focus and I loved that feeling of being in "the zone." I was proud of myself that day, I ran the fastest, shot the best, and proved myself as a force to be reckoned with.

Me, Dad, & Blake at the Atlanta Hoop City
3 on 3 competition

Sweet Sixteen

The first month and a half of school went by quickly. I had become so busy with new friends, keeping up with old friends, and most importantly basketball, that I hadn't even noticed the time passing. I was also growing increasingly worried that my old school's basketball team was going to challenge my eligibility. I didn't live in the same district as the high school that I was attending, so if I was challenged, I wouldn't be eligible to play for an entire year. My parents and I had been looking for a house in the district of my new school, Curry. We had to move quickly so I could play basketball, or my whole reason for changing schools would be destroyed.

However, the worry over my eligibility was overshadowed by the excitement of my sixteenth birthday. There were only a couple of weeks before it rolled around, and my parents had joked that my gift would be a new house in my school district. Like most other sixteen-year-old young men, I couldn't wait to get my license and experience that first taste of freedom. Around this time in my life, I started feeling tired quite often and I was easily fatigued during basketball practice. My mom asked me one day after I had had a rough basketball practice, her usual, "How was practice?"

I responded, "It sucked, I feel like instead of getting better, I'm getting worse." I felt like I couldn't run as fast as I could just a few weeks before and I was losing some of my spark. My mom said it was because I had been working out so much and not sleeping enough. My life was very hectic at the time and I was under stress. I figured she was probably right.

I kept up my usual activities as I looked forward to my sixteenth birthday. I had made a lot of friends in the short two months I had been attending my new high school. One of them, a girl I had gotten to know, had just found out she had cancer. She was diagnosed with Hodgkin's lymphoma. I couldn't believe it. I felt so bad for her and her family. I remembered wondering how something so awful could happen to someone so wonderful. This girl, her name is Sarah, had just come back from Hollywood, she could sing and dance and act and she was really sweet. She had so much going for her; I just couldn't believe that something so horrible could happen to her. I can't explain why, but somehow I felt deeply affected by what Sarah was going through. I guess I was in shock; I had just gotten to know her a few weeks earlier when we went to the fair with mutual friends. We clicked immediately and I had looked forward to spending more time with her. I'll never forget the day I found out, October 18, 2008. She had been diagnosed two days before, on the sixteenth. A friend of mine called me and told me the news about Sarah, my heart sunk. You don't expect someone who is sixteen and healthy to get cancer. When she was diagnosed, I researched the cancer she had and I knew what her survival chances were, she was in one of the final stages of the disease. Death became so real to me then.

My sister came back home to visit the weekend I found out about Sarah. She had made plans to take our little brother, Chan, and me to the pumpkin patch in our hometown since it was getting close to Halloween. I couldn't help but get excited when she and Blake came home; I liked having them home because it felt like a missing piece of our family was back and somehow I felt more whole.

I wasn't home the Friday night Tab arrived. I had already made plans to stay with a new friend that night, but I was excited about our pumpkin patch adventure and would be sure to come home as soon as I woke up the next morning.

I woke up Saturday morning because someone was shaking me. I opened my eyes to see the friend that I had spent the night with standing over me and telling me urgently that I had to get up because I had to get to the pumpkin patch. I jumped up eagerly and had him drive me home. The first person I saw as I walked up to our glass garage door that day was my sister. She was all dressed up and ready for our outing.

"You ready to go to the Pumpkin Patch?" She asked me in a sweet baby voice. It's funny how even though I was about to be sixteen, she treated me like I was still really little.

"Yeah, are you?"

"Almost." She sat down across from me at the kitchen table with a plate of food and a drink. We talked for a while and caught up while she ate. I told her about school and basketball and the houses Mom, Dad, and I had found in my new school district. She ended up looking at my yearbook from my freshman year when I was still at Walker High School, the same high school she and Blake had attended. She skipped around quickly wanting to see the pictures of me as class president and class favorite, and she also eagerly flipped to the basketball section. As she was scanning through the yearbook, I stopped her at a picture. It was Sarah's picture, my heart immediately sunk from the sorrow I felt for her. I grabbed my sister's hand before she could turn the page again, "You see that girl right there."

"Yeah," she looked at me curiously.

"She just came back here to Jasper from Hollywood. She's really nice; I hung out with her earlier this year. She found out that she has cancer; it's called Hodgkin's lymphoma. I just can't believe it. I feel so bad for her."

"That's really sad." My sister said. And that was the last we talked about it.

I had so much fun that day with my big sister and my little brother. I enjoyed riding in my sister's car with the windows down. My big sister's boyfriend joined us on our excursion and he was occupying the front seat, most of the time I would have taken the front seat, but it was fun sitting in the backseat with my little brother. Both of us liked the feel of the wind blowing around us, we felt really free. It made me giggle when I looked over at him and saw how funny he looked with his hair blowing wildly all over his head. I watched him for a while and smiled.

I had prayed for him for a long time. I was the youngest in my family, and my parents had proclaimed that they were done with having children now that they had me and my older siblings were happy with that. However, I felt really strongly about having a little brother, I begged my family and got a resounding "no" as my answer. So, I did the one thing I knew would work, I prayed. About a year later I got my baby brother Chandler, he's my world to say the least.

I looked up to find that we were driving down an old country dirt road; it lasted for a while and then dead-ended into a small grass parking lot. Although my sister wasn't the best driver, we trusted her to always get us to our destination safely, and she had.

I could see the big blow up slides and the hay maze and I could smell hotdogs and popcorn being cooked at the concession stand. I loved places like this, where the only thing you have to do is have fun and there's so many ways to do it.

My big sister and her boyfriend, Chris, and Chandler and I spent the rest of the day enjoying each other and enjoying the beautiful October day we'd been given. We ran through the hay maze over and over again, hiding from each other, tricking each other into going the wrong way and laughing like crazy. We fished with cane poles and Chandler caught a fish on his first cast into the pond. At one point, the four of us were the only ones on the big blow up slide, we would slide down and chase each other back up again, I think my sister and her boyfriend and I were the only somewhat grown up people that played on the slides that day. We finished the day off by picking out pumpkins, Chandler of course got the littlest, cutest one, Tab got the most perfect one she could find by scanning rows and rows until she found the one with the best color and shape. Tab's boyfriend grabbed another small pumpkin that Chandler expressed interest in taking home along with the one he had already picked up. I got the weirdest looking one I could find, the one I knew no one else would look at twice, I wanted to give it a good home.

After a nice dinner at a mom and pop restaurant in our little southern town, we were full and sleepy, so my sister drove us all home. I thought about how wonderful it would be if every day could be like the one we had just had. That day became one of my fondest memories; it was one of my last "normal" family outings.

My sister left that night after the pumpkin patch. I didn't want her to go, I felt that we could talk about things that I couldn't talk to other people about. We shared a special bond that's hard for me to explain, maybe it was because we were the middle children, I'm not sure. Either way, I was sad to see her go, she hugged me tight and kissed me a few times. She knew my birthday was coming up so she had given me tickets to a big concert she was working on in Nashville that was on my birthday. She made me promise that she would see me soon. I was excited to take my first road trip to Nashville with my newly issued license I planned to get the morning of my birthday.

I woke up early on the morning of my sixteenth birthday because I wanted to go get my license before school. My mom was giving me her car and we had also picked out a lake house in my school district to move to so I wouldn't have to worry about my eligibility being challenged anymore. Those were my two big gifts. My cousin, Alex, had come from Kentucky, where both my mom and dad's families are from, to stay with my family for a little while. Since he was there, he drove me to the DMV. We sung along to the radio on our way. I was on cloud nine; it was my first taste of freedom.

I was the only person there that morning to take a driving test, so it didn't take long before I was on the road with a friendly woman jotting notes on a piece of paper attached to a clipboard. Ten minutes later, I officially passed the test. After getting my picture taken and receiving my temporary license, I went on to another day of classes and basketball practice. I was feeling a little sick and had told my dad the day before my symptoms, which included feeling congested and easily fatigued. He gave me oral antibiotics, that he had given me many times before, called Z-Pak to take; assuming that I probably had the same upper respiratory infection I had gotten every year in October since I was born. I didn't feel like the antibiotics were helping, even though I was taking them regularly the way my dad had instructed me too. I was so sick that I texted my sister that day to let her know I wasn't coming to the concert that night. I wanted to take my first long drive to Nashville. I had talked about the day I would be able to do that for so long, but I knew I was too sick. That day at school went by slowly, I was excited about getting my license, but I felt pretty bad, "I must have the flu, I thought." I just wanted to go home and lay in the bed. I drudged through basketball practice and finally made it home.

My brother, Blake, had come home from medical school for my birthday. He gave me a hard time about being our parents' favorite.

"Nobody else gets an awesome car and a house for their birthday." He joked with me.

I smiled at him. I was really glad to see him, but I was feeling exhausted and my lungs had begun hurting from the congestion I had been having. I talked to him for a little while, but not nearly as long as I usually would have and went on upstairs to bed. Even though my birthday was great and all of the things that had been worrying me were finally taken care of, all of the excitement I felt couldn't fight the exhaustion I was feeling. I felt weak as I crawled into bed. I kept myself up coughing for a while, but eventually faded into a deep, heavy sleep.

The Diagnosis

The next morning, I had trouble waking up. I was congested and weak, and even though I had been sleeping for about ten hours, I was still very tired. My alarm clock had gone off for a good thirty minutes before I ever woke up, that was out of character for me. "What's wrong with me?" I wondered as I forced myself up out of bed. I told myself I was just sick, all I had to do was get through this day at school and then I'd have the weekend to recuperate.

I drove myself to school that day even though I wasn't feeling well. In my second class, I started getting chills, severe chills. I was freezing and bundled up in my jacket, even though all of the other kids in my class seemed to be comfortable in light t-shirts. One of my friends, Tyler, offered me his coat, which he wasn't wearing because he felt hot. So, I put it on over the red fleece jacket I was already wearing, but it didn't really help. I went through my next few classes; feeling bad and still wearing the coat my friend had given me.

My sister sent me a text as she usually did during the day while she was at work and I was at school. I guess Mom had told her that I had gotten my license. I looked at my phone under my desk in class; I was still covered in two thick coats. Her text read: "Hey char; I heard you got your license, congratulations! I'll bring you a present when I come home. I love you!"

I texted back a quick, "okay, I love you too." and put my phone away before my teacher noticed it.

Tyler saw me again in my next class and noticed I was still shivering under his coat. He said, "You don't look so good, we should go to the nurse and get your temperature taken."

I agreed and walked with him to the nurse's office. The nurse stuck a plastic covered thermometer in my mouth and when it beeped, it revealed that my temperature was almost 102 degrees. The nurse said I should go home, but I didn't want to miss basketball practice. So, I stuck the rest of the day out and was relieved when practice period rolled around.   I got changed with my teammates, and headed out for practice. I was feeling weaker than I could ever remember feeling before. I was getting winded just from walking up and down the stairs to the locker room. My coach saw me and noticed that I looked quite pale. I told him I hadn't been feeling very well that day, and he sent me home.

When I got home, I went straight upstairs to my bed. I began coughing up fluid so often as I laid and tried to fall asleep that I had to pull the garbage can from my bathroom into my bedroom. I sat it beside me on the floor next to my bed. I slept in between my coughing fits for the next four hours. When I woke up and started coughing up blood, I knew something wasn't right. So, I got myself up and drove myself to my dad's clinic. I called him to let him know what was wrong and that I was on my way.

When I arrived at my dad's urgent care clinic about ten minutes later, I went in the back door. I walked straight to my dad who was standing at the nurse's station, waiting for my arrival. He sat me in a chair in one of the patient rooms and said he would return later. Soon, a nurse came in; she took my temperature and drew some blood samples. When she left, I laid down in the hospital bed across from the chair I was sitting in; it was covered with wax paper. I glanced around the room and studied the different glass jars that contained all of the usual hospital utensils. I remembered how I used to love playing with the tongue compressors when I was younger. Eventually I focused on the TV hanging from the ceiling and I switched it on. It was taking my dad a lot longer than it usually did to come back in the room and let me know what was wrong with me. I started watching TV as I waited for him to return.

A while later my dad came in the room, his face looked very solemn and concerned. "So, do you know what I'm sick with, do I have the flu?" I asked.

He sat down in the seat next to me holding some papers and looked at me. He said, "Charlie, you're white blood cell count is pretty high. You should have, at the most ten thousand white blood cells, and right now, you have eighty thousand. I've only seen a white blood cell count this high twice in my career, and both of the people with the high counts had leukemia. Based on that, I think it could be a possibility that you have leukemia as well. We need to take you to Children's Hospital now. I'm going to stay here and shut down the clinic. Drive yourself home and pack a bag. I'll meet you there."

I just responded with, "Okay." I didn't know what else to say. I was shocked. I just thought he had to be wrong. My mind began to race. I thought, "There's no way I have leukemia, but I guess I should just do what he says. I don't even really know what leukemia is. I know it's cancer, or at least I'm pretty sure it's cancer. It must be pretty bad for Dad to be so concerned."

I drove myself the short ten minutes home, I didn't listen to any music; I just drove and thought. Isn't leukemia what those little kids on the St. Jude's commercials have? None of them have hair; am I going to lose my hair? I wondered if this would affect my basketball career. The season was about to start; and I didn't want to miss very many practices. How long will I be in the hospital? Maybe they'll just see me tonight and send me home tomorrow.

I pulled in my driveway and sat in my car for a moment. I needed to get my thoughts together before I entered the house. I knew if I didn't handle it calmly and quietly, someone would get worried and I didn't want anyone but Blake to know what was going on. I decided that I would grab my basketball bag out of the laundry room and throw a few clean pieces of clothing into it. Since the laundry room was directly to the right when I walked in my house, I knew I would attract as little attention as possible. As I walked into the garage, I saw my big brother sitting in a recliner in our living room through the glass door of our home. I walked into the laundry room to start quickly packing my clothes and called Blake to meet me in there. I didn't want to scare everybody else by what I had to say.

"What is it?" He asked as he came around to face me in the laundry room. I checked around the corner to make sure that my mom or my little brother wasn't within earshot.

"Dad thinks that I might have leukemia. He said my white blood cell count was real high."

"How high was it?"

"I think Dad said eighty-thousand."

He obviously thought Dad was wrong. He said, "Whatever."

"No seriously. Dad's closing the clinic and everything, he's coming over here to get me and take me to Children's Hospital in Birmingham."

Blake went back to the lazy boy recliner he had been sitting in when I first arrived and started playing on his laptop. I found out later that he had been trying to figure out what else besides leukemia could cause a white blood cell count to be extremely high.

I continued packing, worried that my mom would find out before I left. I knew that if anybody told her, she would freak out and I didn't want to be around to see her cry.

My dad pulled in the driveway in his big, black truck; every southern boy's dream car. I hoped that one day he would give it to me. I started walking out to get in the truck with my dad.

"Wait, I'm coming too!" I heard my brother scream as he quickly threw on a pair of shoes.

We hopped in the truck, me in the front seat next to dad and Blake in the back. We began the forty-five minute drive to Children's Hospital in Birmingham. I don't really remember much of what we talked about on the way there. We mostly made light conversation, although we were all a little scared, we didn't exactly know how scared we should be. At one point my dad and brother started talking about the different types of leukemia. They said ALL (acute lymphoid or lymphoblastic leukemia) and AML (acute myeloid leukemia) were the two main types. Most little kids get ALL and most all of them have really high five-year survival rates; which basically meant that they went into remission and didn't develop cancer again in the first five years after treatment.

"Usually," my brother explained, "if you're going to get cancer again after remission, you'll get it within the first five years after you go into remission for the first time. If you stay in remission for those five years than you will more than likely stay in remission for a long time, maybe even the rest of your life."

I think Dad was hoping that if I did have leukemia, I would have ALL. But my brother thought I was too old to have ALL. I got distracted from their conversation for a moment as I rubbed the back of my head. I had had a huge bump back there for a while. It didn't hurt or anything but it still bothered me. Blake broke from the conversation to ask what I was doing.

"I've had this huge bump on the back of my head, right here near my neck." I pointed to show him where, "and I keep trying to pop it or something." He started feeling my head and neck where the bump was.

"That's a swollen lymph node, that's a sign of cancer." He told me. After that, we didn't talk about the cancer much; we just enjoyed each other's company wondering what would happen when we got to the hospital. I tried to call my sister, but got no answer, she must have been out or she would have picked up. I wanted to be the one to tell her what was going on. I texted her and let her know that I was going to Children's Hospital and instructed her to call Dad.

We got to the hospital a lot quicker than I thought we would. We drove around the hospital on the busy Birmingham streets looking for the emergency room. We passed people dressed in Halloween costumes laughing and wandering around in the downtown metropolitan area. Just when I was about to ask my dad if we were lost, my uncle, Perry, called my dad and told him how to get to the parking lot across from the emergency room. Perry told my dad he was waiting there for us. I didn't even know Perry was coming, but it was good to have him around, he was also an urgent care doctor. He had already called the emergency room at the hospital so they knew we were coming, they had an oncology doctor waiting for me. We walked in and signed the sheet they had laying on the metal sill of a glass window. We waited only for a few seconds, not even long enough to sit down, when a nurse came back and told us to follow her. We followed her through the thick metal doors of the emergency room and down the long, sterile hallway, my dad on one side, my big brother on the other and my uncle following closely behind. I smiled a little; they were like guards or fellow soldiers, walking bravely beside me into the uncertainty of a possible war.

I sat down on the small cot-like bed in the room the nurse led us too. My brother sat down in a chair beside me and my dad and uncle pulled chairs into the room to sit on as well. Just as we had situated ourselves, a doctor walked in and introduced herself; I can't remember what her name was. She told us that she was going to draw some blood from me and look at it under a slide with a microscope and basically after that she would let me know if I had leukemia or not. Talk about a long wait. She was gone for about twenty minutes and the four of us, my dad, uncle, brother, and myself sat, talked, and mostly waited for the doctor to come back.

I kept my eyes on the door, and eventually it swung open. I watched the doctor who had left to discover my fate slowly walk back in. I knew what she had seen on that slide before she said anything. When she did speak all she said was, "Well, let's do a little physical and then we'll talk about the plan." The plan. There was the answer. What else would she mean by plan?

She started talking, not to anyone particularly, but to everyone in the room, "I looked at the blood and it does look leukemic from what I can tell. Because I saw Auer rods I believe that it is of the myeloid lineage not the lymphoid lineage." Myeloid. That's the one dad didn't want, wasn't it? The doctor continued to talk for a while longer, but I had stopped listening. When she had finished talking she and my dad stepped outside for a moment before she gave me my physical. Dad and the doctor stood outside speaking to each other quietly for a while. I leaned over to Blake as I watched them whisper, "I'm glad it was me."

"Why?" He asked.

"Because I would much rather be in this bed than you guys. If it was someone else in our family I wouldn't be able to handle it."

Blake hugged me as he began to sob, "I'm sorry this had to happen to you little brother."

When Dad and the doctor returned, Blake left to go pick up the rest of my family. They had gotten the news from Blake once the doctor left the room with Dad and were too shaken up to drive themselves to the hospital. My dad and uncle stayed with me in the emergency room while I received my physical and they discussed treatment options with the doctor. After my physical, I had a short nausea spell and passed out for a moment. When I woke up, I was being wheeled up to the fourth floor of the hospital, the oncology unit.

The staff on the fourth floor had already gotten a room ready for me, room four forty-four. I liked it best out of all of the other rooms, not that I had been in the other rooms, but somehow it felt like it

31

was meant to be my room. It was right across from the nurse's station and was the most noticeable when you walked into the oncology unit. Not to mention that I found it almost like fate because it was room four forty-four on the fourth floor. Even though I liked the room, the shock of my diagnosis was overwhelming, and it was hard to digest that it was serious enough for them to give me a room there in the hospital. None of the doctors or nurses or staff at the hospital could give me any estimate for how long I would be staying in the hospital. I was beginning to realize that I might actually stay there for a night or possibly longer.

Dad and I went into the room, my room. We sat our bags down and looked around the room. At first glance, I just noticed a small hospital bed that I hoped would at least be long enough for me. I also saw on the wall furthest from where we were standing at the door were two chairs, and a large window that covered the entire wall. I knew I didn't pack everything I needed, but then I didn't exactly know what I would need. Everything began to feel very surreal and on top of how sick I was, I knew I needed to lie down. I was feeling exhausted, but the constant flow of hospital staff in and out and the continuous poking and prodding to check on my vitals kept me awake.

My family arrived at the hospital shortly after Dad and I had gotten settled in to room four forty-four. When they walked in, I could tell that they were in just as much shock over my situation as I was. My mom walked in first, followed by Chandler and my cousin, Alex. Blake walked in behind them with his girlfriend. We had two cots pulled out that they used to sit on like couches. The smallness of the room was much more exaggerated with all of us crowded into it together. Just a few hours earlier, all of my family had been out trick or treating with our dogs in our quiet little sub-urban neighborhood while I was sleeping in my room. None of us had any idea that by the end of the night we would be in Children's Hospital and I would have cancer. That first night is bizarre to think about. None of us had any idea what was in store for us and what the real magnitude of my diagnosis was. We laughed and joked together; we were all in denial about what we knew to be true about my condition. Eventually, my family had come and gone and my sister had called crying while she was driving to Birmingham from her home in Nashville. Soon, it was just my dad and me and I faded off to sleep.

I woke up that night and was surprised to be in a small hospital room. Once my eyes adjusted to the dark and my mind adjusted back to reality I remembered the occurrences of the night before. The bed I was laying on was in the center of the room. There was a small flat screen TV hanging on the wall directly across from the bed I was in, next to it was a dry erase board with my nurses name written on it. The name written in blue marker read "Catherine". It was Angela last time I was awake, so I assumed the shifts must have changed while I was sleeping. I really liked Angela, so I was hoping that when I met Catherine I would like her too. I looked around the room, taking everything in. To my right, there was a sink with a mirror over it and a closet was directly to the right of that. The door was also to my right and the bathroom was just beside it. I looked to my left to see my dad lying on a cot next to me. I realized his eyes were open; he was watching me. I noticed the rainbow and smiley face stickers on the head of my bed and on the ceiling, signs of children that came before me. I wondered if they had survived. Then, a still, awareness, came over me. I was struggling to breathe.

Every breath felt like a struggle. The only way to describe the feeling is to compare it to being winded after you've been working out. I had gotten some medication earlier and it was making me groggy. I heard my dad talking with someone, but I couldn't figure out whom he was talking to. I thought maybe it was a doctor, but then I noticed that Dad had buzzed my nurse and was talking to her through the speaker in our room. My dad had realized, before I

even had, that my breathing was labored. Once the nurse was notified, she then contacted the doctor that was on call. The decision
was made to bring a machine into my room. The machine had
what looked like a plastic tube attached to it. They put it over my
head and lifted it over my ears, and then they put the two pieces
that were blowing out air into my nose. It was similar to an oxygen
mask but not quite as powerful, it was called a nasal cannula. They
gave me more medicine and I slowly drifted back to sleep. I felt safe
with my dad laying beside me, watching me sleep.

I slept for most of the next day. The nasal cannula I had on was
bothersome and I struggled to take it off in my sleep. Not only was
I exhausted because of how sick I was, but every moment of sleep I
got was interrupted either by my dad waking me up to fix my nasal
cannula or by a nurse who was there to check my vital signs. My
family came to visit with me sometime in the afternoon, I remember waking up for a moment to say a short, "What's up guys?" but
I stayed sleeping until later in the evening. I was surprised when I
finally woke up, feeling better, to see my family still waiting for me
to wake up. They had to have been there for hours. My whole family was together, and that hadn't happened in a while. We talked and
laughed a lot; I did my best to keep everyone laughing. If I was going to be stuck in the hospital, I might as well make the best of it.

My sister and my mom went to our house in Jasper before I woke
up. They brought back a lot of my personal things and a collage of
pictures of me with family and friends that my sister had made to
hang on my hospital room wall. My sister also bought me new, soft
clothes to wear since there was a possibility that I might be in the
hospital for a while. I loved the clothes, but I hoped I wouldn't be
in the hospital long enough to need them. She also got me house
shoes to wear around the hospital. They felt great and they looked

like my favorite shoes, Wallabees. She hung posters of NBA players on my walls and arranged a large basket of food for me next to my bed. After I had been showered with gifts and the women in my life had fully decorated my room, my sister, always in need of my approval, asked me, "So, what do you think about all the decorating and the new stuff we brought you?"

In an effort to lighten things up, and ready to make my first, but definitely not my last joke about cancer, I said, "I'm thinking I should've got cancer a long time ago!" Everyone laughed, including me, I really liked everything they had done for me. My family went all out to say the least.

My mom brought all of my DVDs for me to watch and everyone in my family put himself or herself at my beck and call. If I even mentioned that I liked something, I would have it within a few hours. I kept telling everyone I was fine and I didn't understand what they were making such a fuss about. Somehow, word had already gotten around to my friends and I was receiving what seemed like hundreds of texts and phone calls. I assured everyone that I was in the hospital, but everything was fine and I was going to be okay. My friend, Sarah, who had been diagnosed just a few weeks earlier, was in the hospital too, on the fifth floor. She had found out about my diagnosis and knew I was in the hospital as well. She brought me a letter that I placed in the drawer of my night stand, but I wasn't ready to read it. Nothing was wrong with me, or at least that's what I kept telling myself. I felt fine.

Soon, however, it became clear with out a shadow of a doubt that I, Charlie Mckinley Lovely, had leukemia. The doctor explained to me, as my dad already had, that leukemia is a disease that affects the white blood cells in the bone marrow. All of the blood cells, red and white, in our bodies are created in the bone marrow. When someone has leukemia, one of the types of their white blood cells isn't reproducing the way it should be and it basically starts mutating out of control and can be fatal. The type

35

of white blood cell that was being affected in me was called a myeloid cell, hence acute myeloid leukemia. The doctor explained that acute means that it progresses quickly and if not caught in time can cause fatality in a matter of days. There it was. It finally sunk in. I felt like I had been hit by a truck.

Blake, Chan, Tab, and I at the
Children's Harbor basketball court.

Chemotherapy, Prepare to Fight

The doctors made their rounds the next day at their usual time. My dad, my big brother and I were all sitting in my hospital room talking when the doctors knocked on my door. My head doctor's name was Dr. Handler; she walked in the room first and was followed by an entourage of other doctors and residents. They had important information for my family and me. I looked over at my dad and big brother. Both of them are big, strong men, but I could see how weak they felt at that moment. They tried to hide it, but I read the worry on their faces. They would be the two men that saw me through this sickness. My brother wouldn't leave my side, and my dad would research the best treatments and call the shots at my hospital stays. I felt safe and comfortable knowing that they were watching over me in everything I went through.

"We would like to start Charlie on chemotherapy in about a week." Dr. Handler began, "We're not in a huge rush, but we want to start fighting this as soon as possible. We will need to give you, Charlie, regular spinal taps in order to check the fluid in your spinal cord to make sure no blasts or leukemia cells have spread to there because if they have, they could be in your brain. We don't think that will be a problem, but for precautionary measures we will go ahead and give you direct chemotherapy there through a small injection in your spinal cord. Because we will need to take so many blood samples and hook you up to IVs, combined with the injections you will be receiving in your back, we feel that it would be best to give you what is called a central line. A central line is a small tube that will be inserted right here in your chest." She touched the area from right under my right shoulder to below my chest on that side. She continued, "The central line will be in your carotid artery and will empty into the superior vena cava. This will give us the best possible place to administer your chemotherapy, so you won't have to go through anymore poking or prodding, besides the spinal cord stuff of course, and you will be able to receive larger doses of your medication. We would also like to hold off on starting chemotherapy to give you and your family time to decide if you would like to join a clinical trial for a new medication that could help your survival rates."

"That sounds pretty good." I said, not really knowing what I should say and not wanting to seem sad or scared so I wouldn't worry anyone. I looked at my dad; he was slouched sitting upright on the cot beside my bed. His head was tilted, so I could tell he was looking at the floor. His thinning hair was tussled on his head where he had been sleeping, he rubbed the stubble on his face that had grown since I had been in the hospital, I could tell he was thinking about my treatment, trying his best to let it all sink in and weighing the options.

He first looked at the doctors and spoke, "I would like to get as much information as possible on the new drug and the clinical trial." Dr. Handler nodded at him.

He looked at me and said, "Now, Charlie, just to prepare you, this central line will come out of your side, there will be two tubes about the length of pencils sticking out at all times, that's where they will draw blood and administer medicine."

"What?" This did not sound so good to me.

Dr. Handler spoke, "That's true, but we will be able to tape them down and they will not get in the way of any normal activities."

"What about basketball?" I said, worried.

"That's something we all need to talk about." My dad began. "Dr. Handler, can you please tell us how long Charlie's first stay will be in the hospital, and after that what precautions we have to take while he's receiving treatment."

"Yes, we do need to talk about that." Dr. Handler began. She never showed any emotion; she was a very slender woman of medium height. She wore thin-rimmed glasses and had short, light-brown hair. Later in my treatment, she would come in my room and talk with me about sports. I came to find out that she knew a lot about sports, especially basketball. She continued with her thoughts on my treatment, "I believe that the amount of time Charlie will need to stay in the hospital during his first treatment will depend on Charlie's response to the chemotherapy. It could be anywhere from thirty to possibly sixty days."

My heart sunk, thirty to sixty days? What does that mean? No school? No basketball? I just sat quietly waiting for her to continue.

"We will discuss more about our hopes and plans and Charlie's treatment at our next meeting. Dr. Lovely, we also need to go over the different options of chemotherapy we think would be best. For now, the plan is to get Charlie's central line in, and prepare him to begin chemo. Once he gets through his first induction, he will need time to build his white blood cell count. When receiving chemotherapy, Charlie, you're immune system will be extremely weak. No one should get in your personal space that isn't wearing gloves or a mask. This means no kissing, hugging, etc. Also everything you wear and touch will need to be as sterile as possible and hand washing will need to be done constantly. You'll learn much more about the hygiene stuff as all of this becomes more familiar to you."

"Can I play basketball?" One of the only two questions I really wanted to know the answers to. The other one was the "am I going to live?" question, but I knew the doctor didn't have the answer for that.

"You can play basketball when you feel well enough and all of your counts are good, but you can't play competitive basketball. It would be too dangerous to have so many other people around you and breathing on you while your immune system is compromised by the chemotherapy. Not to mention the worries of low platelets, if you were to fall or if someone was to hit you, you may not be able to stop bleeding."

I couldn't take in what she was telling me, "So, let me get this straight, I can't play basketball?" She shook her head, "For how long?"

"For as long as it takes to cure you, I can't say an exact amount of time. For the next six months and possibly the next year I would plan on homeschooling and unfortunately no competitive basketball."

"What happens when I'm cured?" I asked. "Is it just over or do I have to continue treatment?"

"Unfortunately, you will have to come back every three months to get your counts checked and make sure that the cancer hasn't returned. This disease is something that is never totally cured, however, you can go in remission and stay in remission. For now, we just have to focus on getting you in remission."

This was a huge blow to me, and gave me another glimpse at how serious my condition was. My life would never be the same; even if I do get better I'll have to constantly worry about the cancer coming back. I'll be in and out of the hospital constantly. I am a cancer patient. I'm a sixteen year old basketball star and class favorite, I have big dreams for my future, and now, I'm a cancer patient. Plain and simple. My world changed. Suddenly everything that I was concerned about a little over forty-eight hours ago didn't matter anymore. Now, I just wanted to live, with out cancer.

Dad continued talking to the doctors about the surgery they would have to do to insert my central line, "What day do you want to do the surgery to put in Charlie's central line?" he asked.

"Tomorrow." Dr. Handler responded.

"Will he be put under anesthesia?"

"We can do the surgery with out anesthesia by using a local anesthetic. However, it's much easier on the child when they are simply put to sleep under regular anesthesia."

"I'm worried about the condition of Charlie's lungs. I understand that he will have to go through intubation to be put under general anesthesia for this surgery and I know that his lungs may not be able to handle the stress of the anesthesia or any possible damage from the intubation." My dad laid all of his worries out on the table for the doctors to take in.

I hoped they would put me to sleep under general anesthesia. I did not want to be awake for the entire surgery, but Dad still had concerns about the condition of my lungs and was fully against me going through intubation for surgery. I knew that intubation meant that they would stick a tube into my lungs to help me breath while I was asleep, I figured that it would be best to take our chances with the little tube than for me to be awake. Dr. Handler told my dad that he could talk to the anesthesiologist before I went in for surgery the next day. Finally, Dr. Handler left, followed by her entourage.

Like clock work, my sister walked in directly behind them. "So, what did the doctors say?" She asked sitting down next to my dad. He didn't answer her. He just sat in silence. I knew that she could see the grief on my face.

"Basically, I'm screwed." I felt defeated and that's exactly how I sounded.

"What?" She said. And that's all it took. I broke down. Everyone else had cried and I really didn't think I was going to. I never cry in front of anyone, I'm the strong one. But right there, in that little bed in room four forty-four, I couldn't stop the tears from coming. I finally realized what all of this meant, I could die. And not just that, not only was my life changed forever, but my entire family, all of their lives are changed forever because of me. I cried over the pain I felt for them, I didn't want to hold them back. I had heard my brother saying he was going to leave medical school to stay closer to me and my sister was going to leave her job to come home as well. I knew how much money this was going to cost Dad. I hated that because of me, their lives were wrecked.

Blake jumped up and hugged me on my left side as I cried, Tab was almost right on top of me with her head laying on my chest, and Dad was on my other side holding me. They held me and cried with me. That's all they could do. Through my tears I said, "I just don't want to hold you guys back."

My big brother looked at me, "Charlie, if one of us were in that bed instead of you, where would you be?"

I looked at him with tears running out of my eyes, he knew I understood. I didn't have to say anything. I would be right where he was, by their side. We continued to cry together, we didn't say anything else. There was nothing else to say.

The sound of my IV beeping woke me up on the day of my surgery. It's funny how I seemed to get less rest in the hospital. When I did fall asleep, I was disturbed at least every two hours because it was time for medicine or the nurse's assistant had to check my vitals. I always liked the nurse's assistants and they always did their best not to wake me up when they came in to take my temperature and my blood pressure. Because of the constant disturbances in the hospital, my sleeping pattern completely changed. Time almost seemed non-existent in the hospital. It was hard to tell if it was light or dark outside, and the hospital had the same amount of light at almost all times of the day. Since my sleeping pattern had gotten off, I never really knew exactly what time it was. I had begun judging the time of day by the nurse's shift changes.

I had already become good friends with the two nurses that had been taking care of me. Angela was my day nurse, she was athletic and had pretty blonde hair that she almost always kept pulled up in a ponytail. I felt extra close to her because she already knew my family through my Uncle Perry who had attended church with her for years. Catherine was my night nurse and she always made me laugh. She reminded me of a mix of my best girl friend, Julianna, and my sister's best guy friend, Scott. I loved when she would just come and hang out in my room for a while if she didn't have to take care of her other patient. Usually my nurses only had me and one other patient at all times so I could pretty much see them all day if I wanted to.

Angela, alerted by the sound of my IV, walked in. So, I assumed it was probably early morning. "Hey Smangela." I said happily.

"Hey Charlie! How are you feeling?" I laughed, I loved the way she said my name. She made it sound so funny.

"Pretty good, but also pretty hungry." The medical staff had made me NPO after 2 AM. Which means that I wasn't allowed to eat anything until after I had my surgery that day. I was going down to have my central line put in that afternoon. NPO stood for nothing per oral. To make sure everyone was aware that I was NPO, one of the nurse's assistants placed a bright orange sign that had NPO in large black font on my door.

"I'm sorry, it's not my call."

"Dang it, I was hoping you would let me slide."

"Nope, I have to look out for your safety." She started messing with my IVs and marked some stuff on the dry erase board hanging in my room.

"Hey Angela, can I ask you a question?"

"Anything."

"Am I going to lose my hair?"

"More than likely, but who needs it anyway?"

"But my hair's like my thing and my head's going to look all weird shaped when it's bald."

"No, you'll look fine."

"You just have a thing for bald kids." I told her.

She laughed and said, "You're right."

I was really worried about losing my hair. I really didn't want to, the thought of seeing my hair fall out made me a little nauseous. I had always had fairly long hair and it was light brown and curly. Supposedly after chemo, my hair would grow back differently, like a different color or texture. Besides not getting to play basketball, this was the next worse thing. It made it even worse that I couldn't do anything about it.

Angela walked out and I decided to sleep until my next interruption. I was anxious about my surgery and really hungry, I rolled over and stared at happy pictures of my family and myself staring back at me. My mom was sleeping on the cot beside me. The rest of my family had gone back to the hotel room they had been renting since I was diagnosed to rest before my surgery. Mom stayed to watch over me through the night and she was still sleeping. I watched her lay there sleeping until I eventually drifted back to sleep.

When I woke up next, one of my doctors was standing over me and talking to my dad. They were preparing to begin my surgery. My dad had been really worried about this procedure since the first talk he had had with my crew of doctors and residents. His worry was that since I was already requiring oxygen to breathe easier that it would be dangerous to put me to sleep. Because my lungs were already so weak, he wasn't sure if I could handle all the stress the anesthesia would put on them. He also knew that in order to do the surgery the medical staff would have to intubate me and he was concerned about the possible injuring of my already weak lungs. He was pushing the doctors to just use a local anesthetic to avoid the risks of intubation, but the doctors kept assuring him that the best option was to put me to sleep.

I guess my dad had finally given up trying to find a way out and the doctors left, they would send someone else up to roll me down to surgery. My dad and I talked for a while about nothing in particular. We watched football on TV. Soon, all of my siblings arrived along with Blake's girlfriend and Tab's boyfriend. "What's up guys?" I said as all five of them tried to cram into my tiny hospital room.

Everyone said their greetings and I got an air hug from Tab, she was practicing for the way she would hug me once my immune system was so bad that she wouldn't be allowed to touch me. I saw that they had brought along Chan as well. "Chan!" I said gleefully.

"Hey Char." He was seven now, but still said my name the same way he did when he was first learning how to talk, it was really funny. He would pronounce the Ch in the beginning of my nickname "Char", like he was saying "Shar."

I could tell that he was a little confused about the whole situation. It seemed that he couldn't' totally grasp what was going on, or he didn't want to. I decided to get out of the hospital bed I had been laying in and sit in the chair to the right of me, pretty soon this chair would have to be sterilized before I was allowed to sit in it. I figured that if I could look as healthy and normal as possible it wouldn't scare Chan so much.

"Chan, come here for a second." He was sitting on one of the two cots in my room beside my sister. I could tell he was apprehensive to move closer to me. I hated that he was so scared. He slowly worked his way around the hospital bed and stood in front of me. We were almost eye to eye, him standing and me sitting. "Come on," I said, "Sit in my lap, it's okay." He tentatively moved forward and sat in my lap. "Now, give me a hug." He hugged me tight around the neck, he was very careful not to pull any of my lines or mess with my nasal cannula. "Do you understand what's going on with me?" I asked him.

"You have cancer." He said. I wondered how his seven-year old mind interpreted what cancer was, I was sixteen and it was almost too much for me to comprehend.

"Yeah, do you know what kind of cancer I have?"

"Leukemia." He said.

"Do you know what that is, like do you know what that means?" I knew there was no way he could.

He shook his head side to side; he had a glum look on his face.

"Well, basically, I'm really sick because my body's way of keeping me healthy isn't working, you know that thing called an immune system?"

He shook his head yes, I knew he understood this, it's hard not to when you grow up surrounded by doctors and medical terminology. "Well, my immune system isn't working the way it should. But the good news is, they have medicine they can give me that will make me better, so it's going to be okay. I'm going to lose my hair and I'll be sick for a little while, but that's it."

"Yeah," he said, his spirit obviously lighter, "And when you start having chemo, I have to wash my hands a lot and be careful about breathing on you!"

I laughed, "Right! Pound it." We always pounded. What we called Pounding was basically bumping your fist against the other person's fist. He got up off my lap and moved back over to the cot. Even though I had talked to him, it was obvious that he wasn't comfortable in the hospital; I can't say I blamed him.

There were seven of us sitting in that little hospital room. Me in the chair beside my bed, Tab's boyfriend, Chris, Tab and Chandler sitting on the folded out cot at the foot of my bed and Blake's girlfriend, Lauren, Blake and my dad sitting on the cot to the left of my bed. We all tried to make light conversation, but we were all really just waiting for surgery time to come. This was one of our first "big days" at the hospital, the implanting of my central line. If you stay in the oncology unit for a while, you get used to certain terms, like "big days." Big days usually consisted of things like surgeries, the beginning or end of a round of chemotherapy, the results of tests coming back, etc.

At a little after noon, there was a knock on the door of my room. "Come in." I called. Two ladies in scrubs and wearing name tags came in and announced they were there to wheel me down to the second floor for my surgery. I didn't see a wheel chair, so I assumed that I would be taking my bed down to surgery with me. I got out of the chair and laid in my bed, everyone else began moving out of the room while my dad and sister moved things around to allow my bed to be wheeled out. Soon, there was one lady behind me, pushing, and the other lady was at my side, they pushed me out of the room and down the hallway to the "staff only" elevators. Everyone else followed behind.

The ladies, who were nurses from the surgery floor, were wheeling me down introduced themselves; one was a very southern older lady. The other was a quiet young African American woman. I liked both of them immediately. I began joking around with these two ladies in scrubs as I introduced myself and everyone else.

"That's my dad, Tim, he's a doctor. He's pretty good I guess." My bed was rolled into the elevator. "And that's my big brother, Blake." The elevator doors closed and we began our slow descent to the second floor. "He's in medical school. That's his girlfriend Lauren, she's alright." The elevator doors opened, revealing a sterile hallway with one painted picture that looked oddly out of place. "And this pretty girl beside me is my sister." My bed was being pushed out of the elevator; we were on the floor my surgery would be done on. My sister's boyfriend was leading the way. The southern, older lady told him to go left, but he went right. "That's my sister's boyfriend, Chris, he's not too smart, but he's pretty good looking so I guess that makes up for it." Everyone laughed. "And that's my little brother Chan, he's seven." The two women smiled at everyone as we walked. They wheeled me down a hallway that was painted in waves of dark blue. Everything in the hall was space themed. There were stars painted in the dark blue waves and astronauts with the faces of children were all around us.

"Here we are." The African American woman at my side said.

They opened the door of one of the pre-surgery hospital rooms and wheeled me in. One of the ladies stayed with me and the other went to get the rest of my surgery crew including the surgeon and the anesthesiologist. Everyone stood in the room around me, my sister held my hand. We didn't wait very long, before my surgeon and anesthesiologist came in. They introduced themselves and were immediately ready to whisk me off to surgery, everyone took turns hugging and kissing me before they had to go sit in the surgery waiting room. My dad tried one last attempt with the anesthesiologist to keep me from having to be intubated for the surgery. In the end, all of the decisions remained the same. My dad kissed my forehead and said he loved me, normally this would have been weird but under the circumstances it was exactly what I needed. He walked out of the room and stood in the hallway with everyone else.

As the surgery team wheeled me out of my pre-surgery room and down the hallway to surgery, I was pounding it with all of them, getting everyone pumped up to get through this surgery. I silently prayed to get myself pumped up for the surgery. Just as I had started to get in the zone for what was about to happen. I heard my mom yelling, "Wait, wait!" The team stopped and I looked around to see my mom running down the hallway towards my hospital bed surrounded by people in scrubs and masks. She grabbed me and hugged me and kissed me a lot and said, "I love you so much Charlie."

"I love you too, Mommy." I always called her mommy when I was sick or hurt. The team wheeled me off and into a bright room. I saw a lot of steel and white and it smelled like alcohol. Soon the anesthesiologist was beside me, giving me an IV of something. She asked me how I was feeling, and I responded with, "tired and dizzy."

"Good, that's how you should be feeling." She said. Soon after, my vision became blurry and soon everything was black.

Intensive Care

I woke up to see the anesthesiologist standing over me, the same place she was just a little earlier before I fell asleep. We were still in the well-sterilized surgery room we had been in before I fell asleep. Was the surgery over? I didn't feel like I had been asleep for very long. I soon realized that I was on a full oxygen mask. I was really out of it as they moved me into a small, curtained off room. A nurse came in with water and ice chips for me; apparently I was still not allowed to eat. Blake and my best friend, Eddie, walked in behind her.

"What's up Eddie?" I said as I lifted the oxygen mask up off of my face so I could talk.

"What's up, man? I brought you some presents, but they wouldn't let me bring them back, so I guess you'll have to wait until you go back to your room on the fourth floor."

"Yeah, if they don't give it away."

"They're not going to give your room away." My sister announced as she walked into my little curtained room. Only two people were allowed back at a time, but she never paid attention to those rules.

"Yeah, they will."

"Char, don't worry about it. I promise that you'll go back to room four forty-four. They won't take that room away from you if Angela and Catherine have anything to do with it."

"I really hope I get to go back to it." I knew that my nurses would do all they could to keep my room for me, but if another kid needed it, they would have to give it away. I didn't want to lose room four forty-four; it was my room.

"Hey Char, me and Blake are going to step out for a minute so that you and Eddie can hang out alone for a little while." My sister said. She pulled the curtain to the side and Blake followed her out. I wondered why they were really leaving, I knew Tab well enough to know she wanted to tell Blake something that she didn't want me to hear and that was the real reason why her and Blake were stepping out.

Eddie and I didn't have much time alone because my parents soon appeared in my little curtained off room. My dad explained that the doctors had decided to take me down to PICU or the pediatric intensive care unit right away. Apparently, while I was in surgery, they rolled me on my side to do a bone marrow biopsy and when they did, all of my vitals dropped really low, especially my oxygen saturation, that's why I was on an oxygen mask, but I felt okay. My dad's fears of my weak lungs had been confirmed. My lungs were now so weak that I was getting even less oxygen on my own. I looked over at my mom and noticed it looked like she had been crying. Now I knew what Tab and Blake were talking about, but then Dad continued to talk.

"There is another reason for them taking you to PICU. Do you remember what your white blood cell count was at the clinic?"

How could I forget? "It was 80,000." I said.

"Well, while you were in surgery that count jumped up to a little over 100,000. Charlie, that's dangerously high so when they come to take you to the PICU, your mother, big sister, and I will go discuss your chemotherapy with Dr. Handler. I think they'll want to start almost immediately. Blake is going to stay with you."

"Okay, so what's going to happen in intensive care?"

"I'm not quite sure, as soon as I talk with Dr. Handler I'll come to you and let you know what's happening."

"Alright. Are you guys going to go talk to Dr. Handler now?"

"Yeah, and we'll see you in the PICU in a few minutes."

They hugged me and kissed me and they told me they loved

me. Tab stepped back in with Blake just long enough to kiss my sweaty forehead and give me her love. Soon I was being wheeled out of my little curtain room to the pediatric intensive care unit. The nurse took me back to the staff only elevator that I had come down on just a few hours earlier, but this time there were only two people with me, a nurse and my brother. She took me to the third floor and wheeled me into yet another small curtained off room. She told my brother and I that it would only be a temporary room until after the doctors consulted with my parents. I felt pretty tired and told Blake, he said it'd probably be good for me to get some rest. I closed my eyes and feel asleep to the beeping of the machines that had now begun to sound familiar.

I don't know how long I had been lying in that little blue curtained off room. At least I had been in my same bed the whole time. It's funny that somehow being in the same bed made me more comfortable. It was my bed with my egg crate mattress cover and my sheets that smell like home, and my grandmother made the blanket I was laying under. It was comforting to have a piece of home with me.

I looked over and where my brother had been sitting now sat my dad, and my mom was sitting beside him. My sister was standing behind them. My mother was crying, I was really weak and it hurt me too much to see her cry. I mustered up all the strength I could and raised my index finger with the pulsar that kept track of my heartbeat attached to it and pointed it at her, "Don't cry." I said in the sternest tone I had ever taken with my mother. She immediately stopped. I don't know if it was because she didn't know I was awake or because she would do anything I said at that moment. I knew why they were there; they were going to tell me what Dr. Handler said.

"We're just going to be in this little room for a few more minutes, they're going to move you to a more protected room because you're immune system is weak and will continue to get weaker."

"So, when am I going back to my room on the fourth floor?"

"I don't know, maybe a couple of days."

"Aw man, they're going to give it away." No one said anything. I assumed it was because that was the least of their worries, but it was the only thing that I felt I had even just a little bit of control over, so I stayed focused on getting my room back. Before my dad could finish talking to me, a nurse came in and explained to my sister that only two people could be with a visitor at one time. She had already gotten that lecture, but let it go in one ear and out the other. My sister told me she would be back and walked out to the waiting room.

The nurse then prepared me to be moved to my actual room. She wheeled my bed through the cramped PICU. There were small curtained off sections on either side of me. There were two nurse's stations in the center of the PICU and in front of the one nearest me I saw two small glass rooms. I was wheeled into one of them, I saw the number of the room as I was being wheeled in, room thirteen.

"No! You guys are putting me in thirteen?" I said joking with the nurse and holding onto either side of the door so that she couldn't push me in any further. The nurse laughed.

"Nah, I'm just kidding." I said as I released the door frame and allowed her to wheel me on into room thirteen. "My room on the fourth floor is four-forty-four," I continued talking to the nurse as she positioned my bed in the room; she smiled at me as she listened. "Hey! Four, Thirteen, I know what that means! Philippians four, thirteen, 'I can do all things through Christ which strengthens me.' My favorite Bible verse!" I smiled at the nurse as she smiled back at me. I took my current observation as a sign from the Great Physician. I knew he was protecting me and that

I would be okay. I felt peace and happiness, even though my circumstances wouldn't normally arouse such emotions.

After the nurse got all of my machines and IVs in order, my dad began telling me what Dr. Handler had decided. Most of what he said, I had already figured out on my own by listening to the doctors and nurses going over my chart while they stood outside of my little glass room and consulted one another as the nurse positioned me in my room. Dad explained to me that the head doctor on my case, Dr. Handler, wanted to start chemotherapy on me that night. The doctors had been holding off on starting my chemotherapy because they were going to put me in a clinical trial that could possibly increase my survival rates. However, my condition had made a turn for the worst rapidly after surgery. My dad's fear had become a reality; I had incurred a pulmonary hemorrhage during surgery through the intubation process. The doctors had taken an x-ray of my lungs after surgery before I woke up since I was having trouble keeping my oxygen saturations up on my own. The blood from the pulmonary hemorrhage combined with the sludging that had already occurred in my lungs from the build up of blasts or leukemic cells resulted in what looked to be an ARDS picture x-ray. ARDS stands for acute respiratory distress syndrome. ARDS is a very serious condition and has a fairly high risk of fatality.

I didn't respond to everything my dad had just laid out for me, I didn't need to; I just had to do what I had to do. As I was soaking in the news, one of the doctors on my case came in to talk. His name was Dr. Hurst, I bonded with him because he had been a college basketball player and loved the game as much as me. Automatically we had a lot in common. He mentioned to my dad that Red Cross had a machine that could possibly help my white blood cell count. My dad was immediately intrigued. He began to drill the doctor for information on this machine. I didn't say anything I just watched my dad and this doctor go back and forth with medical terminology that at times went above my head.

Apparently, there was a procedure called leukapheresis. During leukapheresis, there would be a machine that would be attached to me through tubes inserted inside my leg. These tubes would carry my blood through the machine and through a filter. Because the leukemia cells were not fully developed, they were much larger than the healthy white blood cells. So, the leukemia cells would get caught in the filter and only the healthy cells would circulate back into my body. The process of leukapheresis is very similar to the process of dialysis.

"What are the side effects and the risk factors?" My dad asked as soon as the doctor finished explaining to him the general idea of leukapheresis.

"Well it can lead to shortness of breath, vision changes, and there is a small risk, as with most medical procedures, that other organs could be damaged. I really don't think that Charlie would have any difficulties with it, but I can't say for sure because I haven't seen it used often. However, I would tell you, if Charlie were my son, I would do it. If he responds well, he will have a much lower white blood cell count and it will help him recover more quickly. You should be aware that the count could go down and then rebound to as high as it is now or maybe even higher. There's really no way of knowing how it will turn out, but Charlie's a very sick kid right now, and anything that could help him recover is a good thing."

Having a doctor, especially Dr. Hurst, say just how sick I was made me realize that there was a chance I could die, not in a few months or a few years, but possibly just a few hours or a few days. Then my dad said, "How soon can we start leukapheresis?"

"We can give Red Cross a call now and see if they have a machine available, if they do then it will just depend on how long it takes for them to transport the machine from their offices to the hospital."

My Uncle Perry had walked in to my little glass room in the PICU just as Dr. Hurst finished speaking. My dad explained what he and Dr. Hurst had been talking about. My dad, Dr. Hurst, and my uncle began a short conversation. I wasn't really listening, I felt like they kept repeating the same things. My dad and my uncle were rubbing their face stubble as they weighed the pros and cons of this procedure. My uncle finally said, "I think it sounds like something we should try." My dad agreed, and the doctor hurried off to contact the Red Cross.

I sat in my glass room with my dad waiting for Dr. Hurst to return and tell us what the Red Cross had said and if I would be able to do leukapheresis. I stared at the two double doors leading into PICU where visitors entered and left. Dad's spirits were much higher than they had been; I think the leukapheresis procedure had shined a glimmer of hope into his medical mind. He smiled at me and coached me along. "Just look at it like a basketball game, we're down at the half, but not by much. And our competitor is good, but not as good as us." I smiled and nodded my head at what he told me. I liked looking at it that way. I was still staring at the double doors waiting for Dr. Hurst to return when one of the doors swung open. I was sure it would be Dr. Hurst, but it wasn't. I noticed, in excitement and shock, that not only was it not Dr. Hurst, it was my mom's sister, my Aunt Barbara. I watched her as she washed her hands thoroughly and hurried back to my room. It lifted my spirits tremendously to see her; she had always been like another mother to me. She walked in the room with the biggest, most beautiful smile I had ever seen, "What have they been doing to my Charlie?" She said as she rushed over to hug me. She told me that my Uncle David and his entire family had also traveled the eight hours from Kentucky, where my entire extended family lived, to see me as soon as they heard I was sick. She didn't stay back in my glass room with me for long. She told me that everyone wanted to have a chance to see me while I was feeling well, and before the doctors started my treatment. The more family I heard was there, the better I felt. I grinned under my oxygen mask, waiting to greet the rest of my family that had traveled so far to support me. One by one I watched my family members come and go through the two double PICU doors. It didn't take long, however, for Dr. Hurst to return.

"I've spoken with the Red Cross. They have a machine available and are on their way with it as we speak. Once they get here, we'll get Charlie hooked up. It may take about twenty minutes or so to get him connected to the machine, during that time we won't allow visitors to be back here. After he's hooked up, we will come and get you." Dr. Hurst spoke to my dad, I felt like a little kid, not welcome in grown up conversation, but this conversation was about me.

"Sounds good. Thank you." My dad said as he sat beside me. My mom, sister, and my Aunt Barbara, and Blake all took turns visiting me while they still had the chance. When the machine got there, they would all have to be in the waiting room. I thought about what it would be like to be in their shoes. Sitting out in the waiting room for two hours every other two-hour interval, waiting to get a phone call or hear about my progress from a doctor or nurse. Then having to take turns to come see me two at a time during the short two hours they were allowed to come see me. I didn't like being back in that glass room with out them, and I know they hated not being back there with me.

The machine arrived quicker than anyone expected, including me. The machine technician, some doctors, and some nurses were all in my room. A nurse explained that she was giving me a drug called ketamine; she explained that it would put me to sleep for a little while. I knew that I was in a very dangerous situation and I honestly didn't know if I would wake up again. Before I faded off to sleep, I decided that all there was left to do was hope for the best and prepare for the worst.

The next thing I knew, I was a red blood cell flowing through the tubes of the leukepheresis machine. I was in my body and I could see all of my healthy white blood cells and all of my leukemia or blasts cells. The other red blood cells and I swam, almost racing each other through veins and out into a tube, twisting and turning. Soon, I had somehow gotten bigger and I was wiggling to get through the tubes. The tubes went around and around, I was being turned upside down, it was like an intense roller coaster ride that I couldn't get off of. As I made the descent through the twisty tubes, about to be returned back into my body, I flipped myself around so that I was facing the filter of the leukapheresis machine.

I saw the leukemia cells getting trapped there. They looked like morbidly obese babies, like smaller fatter versions of the Buddha. They were all getting caught up in the filter, but kept moving trying to get through. I was trying to hold myself in position in the tube, trying to keep them from coming back into my body, they looked at me wiggling their disgusting little bodies and laughing at me, taunting me. They laughed, "Ah, He, Ha." They all had the same laugh, I heard it over and over again from all of them, there were thousands piling up on top of each other with no where to go, laughing. "Ah, he, ha. Ah, he, ha. Ah, he, ha…."

I came to and saw Dad and Blake standing beside my bed. I was in a hospital gown that was pulled up off of my legs and down off of my chest. There was a box fan blowing on me, and an oxygen mask on my face. I looked over and saw the big leukapheresis machine with tubes all over it and my blood running through them. I saw the machine technician sitting their taking notes. My dad realized that I was waking up and told me that I had spiked a fever and that was why they had pulled my hospital gown down and turned the fan on. They had also laid wet, cold cloths on my chest to help break my fever. I knew that it was usually considered a bad sign for someone in my condition to spike a fever, but I felt so horrible, I didn't care.

"Oh my gosh. Oh my gosh." I muttered.

"What's wrong?" My dad asked alarmed.

"I feel sick, I feel like I'm on a roller coaster and I can't get off." I had never felt so horrible; it was indescribable. My dad immediately alarmed the nurse and the doctor. Apparently, I was having a reaction to the anesthesia called ketamine that they gave me. The nurse explained to me that the side effects of ketamine can be similar to the side effects of PCP. I explained what I was feeling and she agreed that it was similar to the side effects of PCP. So, they gave me another drug to counter act the effects of the ketamine. It was at that moment that I realized I had no desire to ever try any drug, ever.

As the new medicine made its way through my veins, the effects of the ketamine began to subside. I slowly started to come off of my invisible roller coaster. I was so thankful to have that feeling going away. After I started feeling better, my sister came in the room. She started talking to Blake. I must have been out of it from the drugs, because at first I wondered why she didn't speak to me, and then I realized that my eyes had been closed and I had been half way asleep. I looked over eager to bestow upon her my new wisdom in the world of drugs, "Tab, don't ever do PCP." I said lifting the oxygen mask up off of my face so that she could hear me, I felt a little winded and when my words came out it sounds like I had just stopped running before I spoke.

She laughed and said, "Why?"

"It's no good trust me, I just had some."

"They gave you PCP?" She said, obviously confused.

"No," I said laughing. "They gave me a drug called ketamine." I looked at her to make sure she understood what I was saying. "The nurse told me it was like PCP."

"Are you kidding me? How did it make you feel?"

"I felt like I was on a crazy roller coaster that I couldn't get off of. It was horrible. Oh my gosh. I'm so glad it's over. Don't ever do it, trust me."

"Okay." She said laughing. It didn't matter what I said, she always laughed.

I thought about the time we were up late at night sitting in the living room of the house we grew up in, talking to each other as we had so many nights before and as we did so many nights after. Every time I said something she would laugh hysterically. "Why do you laugh at everything I say?" I said, even though the sound of her out of control laughter was making me laugh.

"Because you're funny she said." Still laughing.

"You're WBC, which is your white blood cell count, I think I may have already told you that, is down to 130,00, it was like 178,000. So, that's like a huge decline, better than we even expected for the first count check after beginning leukapheresis. So, you're responding really well to the leukapheresis. There is a chance that you might rebound, but we just have to wait and see. Right now, though, I'm really optimistic." My big brother was almost giddy as he explained all of this to me. I looked at it, since the talk I had with my dad, like it was a basketball game and at that moment, Blake was coaching me. He treated me like his most valuable player, his only player, giving me the odds and pushing me forward. My brother and I were so different, even though we though we had a lot in common. He liked video games and studied odds. He had a very analytical mind. I would rather be playing sports or the drums then looking at a computer screen, unless I was checking facebook or MySpace and I would prefer to never know the odds, I never wanted to get trapped in what the odds were. I believed that every person had unique odds that couldn't be determined and you just had to take the ride, and be unafraid of the outcome. Blake wanted to determine what was in store, but I had already figured out that life couldn't be determined. I had to admit, though, he did a good job of keeping me optimistic.

As he talked I lifted up my oxygen mask so I could eat some ice chips and drink some water, I couldn't remember the last time I had eaten real food. It seemed like days, but I wasn't that hungry. I looked over at the machine and remembered the crazy experience I had when they hooked me up and gave me the ketamine that caused my reaction. I interrupted Blake to tell him what had happened to me while I was under the anesthesia. I talked about the morbidly obese leukemia cells and how I was a red blood cell wiggling through the tubes of the leukapheresis machine. He told me that my mind had created a really good interpretation of what was going on and explained to me why. He always gave really detailed explanations. I listened to him go deeper into his explanation, but exhaustion soon settled in. I was still coming down off of the ketamine, but I felt so much better. I began dozing off, my brother realized how tired I had become and stopped his explanation by saying, "Yeah buddy, you need to get some rest." He patted my arm as he sat beside me. I let my eyes close and faded into sleep.

I woke up and Blake wasn't in my room anymore. I saw my dad sitting in the chair beside my bed, "Dad, go get Blake."

"Go get Blake?"

"Yeah."

"Okay." He got up and walked out immediately. Ever since I got sick, every one was doing anything I asked them to do. It was kind of weird, but it was nice.

Soon, I saw Blake walk through the double doors that lead into the pediatric intensive care unit. I sat in my glass room and watched him thoroughly wash his hands before he continued into my sealed off, glass room. I felt like I was the boy in the plastic bubble.

"What's up brother?" he walked in rubbing antibacterial liquid on his hands. He walked to the side of my bed and laid his hand on my arm. I gently grabbed is hand with mine and looked up at him.

"I just wanted to hold your hand." I told him. I saw the tears well in his eyes. With my hand in his, I felt safe. I peacefully fell back to sleep.

I had been in the glass room, room thirteen, in the pediatric intensive care unit at Children's Hospital for a couple of days now. My vitals were improving greatly each day. The leukapheresis procedure helped my white blood cell count get down to almost normal, and I never rebounded which seemed amazing to everyone. Because my white blood cell count was not as high, I was feeling better. My lungs had been weak from my surgery and they had obviously begun healing because I required less oxygen and was not having much trouble breathing on my own. My heart rate was good, my blood pressure was good, and my fever had gone down. My brother had called my cell phone from the waiting room last night and shared great news. The type of leukemia I had, AML, had different subtypes. The subtypes could have a thirty percent chance of survival, or up to as much as an eighty percent chance of survival. Depending on which one I had; my condition would be favorable or not favorable. The subtype my doctor thought I had was in the favorable category and because of my age and health my, odds were great, maybe even more than eighty percent.

I could tell it was early afternoon by the amount of sun sneaking through the cracks of the closed blinds over my head. I felt alive; I knew it wasn't visiting hours because none of my family was with me in my little glass room. I felt at peace there now, though. I knew that I would be getting back to my room on the fourth floor soon. I closed my eyes and thanked God for bringing me through this trial and asked for strength to make it through the next one.

Official Cancer Patient

After four days in the PICU, I was wheeled back up to the fourth floor and back into room four forty-four. My sister had been right when she told me my nurses would keep it for me. All of my posters were still hanging on the walls where my sister had put them days earlier. My pictures were still sitting on my windowsill, and the collage my sister made me still hung on the wall across from my bed. I felt like I was home, finally.

Angela, the very first person that took care of me in the hospital, was working that day and was finally my nurse again. I loved the nurses in PICU, but I had been able to get so much closer to my four tower nurses. The entire four tower nursing staff cheered for me as my bed was wheeled down the blue and white hallways and back into my room. It was a great homecoming.

My mom's brother David, his wife, Sherry and their three children Josh, Brad, and Austin had come from Kentucky to see me while I was in PICU. I had been able to visit with them shortly before my leukapheresis procedure. I was hoping to see them again, and was happy they were still at the hospital when I was moved back into my old room. My mom's sister, Barbara, was still there as well. Needless to say, I had an entourage taking me to my room. It felt good. I felt almost like a hero coming back from battle, I had won. Victory was sweet, but I new that this was only one battle in a large war. I let myself enjoy the day and the happiness exuding from everyone around me, happiness that my being alive had brought them. I hoped I didn't disappoint them later.

Most of the day was spent talking and laughing with my family. My Aunt Barbara had made potato salad for me; everyone knew potato salad was my favorite dish. We all ate together in my hospital room. I wished I could enjoy the potato salad, but for some reason ever since I had started chemo my first night in PICU, food tasted different. I started feeling sick and when my family noticed; everyone decided it was time to leave. My Aunt and Uncle were going back to Kentucky; it felt like they didn't stay for very long.

Everyone slowly filtered out, and soon it was just my brother Blake and my mom left in room four forty-four with me. Mom was sleeping on one of the cots. Blake was quietly working on his computer on the other cot; I fell asleep to the sound of his keyboard clicking.

I woke up sometime later in the night. I lay in bed looking at the walls around me. I studied everything in the room. I stared at the ceiling slowly going over each sticker that had been placed there by patients in the past. I looked to my left where my brother lay sleeping. Over him was a window that spanned the entire wall. I stared at the window for a few minutes, studying the structure, the blinds, and the posters hanging on one side of them. I've been here before. I knew it, I don't know how I knew it, but I knew I had been there before.

I knew exactly what the view was outside of the window, but since I had been in the hospital, I hadn't looked out of that window. I knew there was a large, plain looking building with steel walls. I knew that sitting in front of that building were two cars: a silver jeep, and a red ford escort. I knew it, with out a doubt. I knew what was out there. I have no idea how I knew. I looked at my mom sleeping on the cot at the foot of my bed.

"Mom." I said into the darkness in a slight whisper.

"What's wrong?" She asked sitting up and looking at me.

"Will you look out that window and tell me if you see a large, plain looking building with steel walls?" She didn't ask any questions, she just stood up and walked to the window. She slowly opened the blinds. I watched and listened as she looked out and described a large, plain looking building with steel walls.

"What kinds of cars are parked in front of it? Is it a silver jeep and a red ford escort?" I asked. She looked out and described a silver jeep and a red ford escort.

"Okay, thanks."

"Why did you want me to tell you what was outside of that window if you already knew what was out there?" My mom asked, sounding a little worried.

"I've never looked out that window, but I've been here before. I know I have."

I quickly got used to my new home in the hospital. As days went by, my family got more adapted to our new way of living and soon we had a system planned out. Each person in the family had a specific job. Mine was to fight my cancer, so that's what I did. Blake stayed with me at the hospital constantly. Everything I did, he did too. When I received each dose of chemotherapy, he was there, standing beside me watching everything the nurse did. Every time I ate, he ate too. I was never alone because my big brother was always there beside me. I knew how I blessed I was to have a big brother that took every step of this new and unusual journey I was on right along with me. I saw many of the other kids on my floor pushing their IVs around the hallways by themselves. I even watched them walk to the lunchroom by themselves to get food. I loved my brother and the family I had, they were willing to lay everything on the line for me, no matter what it was, and I was willing to do the same for them. My brother kept me excited about what each new day in my treatment would hold. Every day I lived and got healthier was a huge boost to my confidence and helped me hold on to hope that I would beat this disease, my brother felt the same way too. We looked forward to hearing my counts everyday. Blake would get them from one of the nurses and read them out loud to me, explaining the positives and sometimes negatives of each.

Living in the hospital as a patient with leukemia your counts are the biggest news you get all day. Your counts are the amount of a certain type of blood cell that you have. If I had a lot of good white blood cells in my counts than I was doing good and I felt good. If my platelets were high enough, Blake and I could go to the activities center in the hospital and play basketball. I usually got at least four to five phone calls from family everyday checking on my counts. When my counts were good, everyone celebrated with me. When they were bad, everyone always seemed to find a positive way of looking at it and helped me focus on making them better next time I had my blood drawn. Usually, if my counts were all pretty low, I couldn't leave my room and visitors wore gowns, gloves, and masks.

My dad usually stayed at a hotel right next to the hospital and spent most of the day with me. He talked to the doctors and researched treatments that would be best for me, he was disappointed when he found out that I couldn't participate in the new drug trial the doctors had gotten us interested in much earlier in my treatment. Because I had to start chemotherapy much earlier than expected in the intensive care unit. We couldn't find any more trials that I could participate in, so all I had was the standard chemotherapy to take and we just had to hope that it would keep me alive. My mom drove back and forth from our home in Jasper to see me at the hospital in Birmingham. She cleaned the house and took care of Chandler. Tab washed my blankets and clothes and showed up everyday with a new basket full of clean amenities. Soon, she would take over driving Chandler to school so my mother could spend more time with me. Mom and Tab were also busy sanitizing our home so it would be safe for me to come home to.

Everyone had their job and we each did what we had to do. I was sad that we didn't get to spend as much time together as a whole, but in all reality, we were spending more time together than ever before.

When I began my stay at the hospital, I didn't know what to expect. My family didn't either. My mommy brought my DVD case to me the second day I was in the hospital; the same day my sister decorated my room. So, for the first week after getting out of PICU, I spent a lot of time watching the many DVDs my family and I had collected through the years.

When I felt good, Blake and I went down to Children's Harbor. Children's Harbor is on the second floor of the hospital and on the other side of a crosswalk. The crosswalk was all glass so the times I walked across it, was really the only time I could see what it looked like outside. Before we went, I would slide on the house shoes my sister got me and put my mask on. Blake would get a wheel chair for me. Most of the time, I had to ride in a wheel chair because my counts were so low as compared to what a normal person would have. Even when my counts were "good", they were low. My counts being low meant a lot of things, mostly, I got tired really easily.

When Blake and I got to go to the harbor, we always had fun. Before I got cancer I was always going places, doing things and spending time with friends, so going to the harbor helped me feel a little more like myself. They had a small, indoor basketball court, a ping-pong table, checkers, and a lot of other things, but the three listed were my favorite. I still loved playing basketball, but I got tired so easily that after a few minutes I had to go sit back down in my wheel chair. So, Blake and I started playing a lot of ping-pong. Sometimes we would play ten to fifteen games back to back. When Tab came, we would play checkers together.

My family wanted me to be as comfortable as possible and part of that meant keeping me entertained. I had realized almost immediately after I was diagnosed just how far my family was willing to go for me. If I even mentioned that I thought something was cool, I had it within a few hours. One evening, a package came to my room. My dad and brother had decided that I needed a good computer to stay connected with friends and play games on. When I opened the package that contained my new computer, I didn't even know what to do with it. It was a huge, top of the line laptop.

"This thing is high tech! I didn't need all this." I said. I was thankful for the gift, but I didn't want my family spending so much money on me. Things aren't important to me.

"Yeah, it's like the best one out now. You'll be able to do anything and everything on this computer. I'll get it all set up for you, so you don't have to worry about it." I saw how much joy my brother was getting out of being able to set up my new gift.

"You like it?" My dad asked smiling from ear to ear. I knew how much he loved to give gifts; his favorite part was the happiness it brought to the person receiving it.

"Yeah, it's awesome, I can't wait to play with it." I really did love it, but I couldn't help thinking about how much my medical bills were already costing my dad, I didn't want to put this kind of stress on my family. I also thought about the other children on my floor that weren't as fortunate as me. I wished they could have what my family had been able to give me. I wanted to help them too. I had talked to my friend, Sarah, who I have mentioned earlier, that had been diagnosed with cancer right before me about the special treatment I received from my family. We spoke mostly through texts, and all of her texts were similar to mine. We were going through the same thing. Her family had begun treating her the way mine had done me, laying everything on the line to make sure each day she had was as good at they could make it. We knew that our families reacted in fear over our survival and we felt a responsibility to fight this disease as hard as possible, if not for ourselves, than for our families. No matter how bad we felt. No matter how much we felt like giving up, we thought about our families to give us strength and perseverance and leaned upon each other for comfort.

It was getting late and after seeing me open my new computer, Dad was ready to go to the hotel and get some rest. Blake and I were alone; I pretended to watch TV as Blake continued working on setting up my computer. I kept thinking about all of the other children in the hospital. I thought about Sarah and what she was going through. We had been texting each other daily as we were both receiving chemo. We could understand what each other was going through better than anyone else. It was nice to have a battle partner. Even though our cancers were different we were still having similar experiences. Because of her, I knew that what was happening to us wasn't just a sad coincidence. God had a plan for us, even though we hadn't yet realized what it was. Sarah and I had been diagnosed only two weeks apart, and for whatever reason God had allowed us to meet right before we found out. As weird as it sounds, it seemed meant to be.

Sarah and I were both blessed to have families that took care of us to the fullest. We were never alone and had everything we needed. We were getting the best care possible. I couldn't help but think about the children I had seen walking around the hospital alone. I couldn't help but think about the rooms I had passed where I saw children younger than Chandler laying in a hospital room with nothing on the walls, no games to play, and no one to play with. How could I help them? I knew I had to do something.

My thought process was interrupted when Angela, my nurse, walked in my room.

"What's up Smangela?" I said joking with her.

"I'm checking on you Charlie." She said, in the funny way she always did. I giggled at her.

"So, be honest with me, am I all of the nurse's favorite patient up here or what?" I smiled at her to make sure she answered with yes.

"Well, you're tied with one other kid."

"Who? I need to meet this kid!"

She laughed, "Actually, I do think you two need to meet. You're the ones all of us fight over. Her name is Hannah Grace."

"Hannah Grace, huh?" I responded, "How old is she and what kind of cancer does she have?"

"She is two and she has a brain tumor. She's been in and out of here since May so we've gotten to know her pretty well. I'll tell her family about you and maybe you can meet her."

"Okay, now?"

"Yeah, her dad is actually wheeling her around the floor right now in her wagon. Hold on a sec."

"Okay." I smiled at her. I wanted to meet this little Hannah Grace.

Before I knew it a man of medium height with dark hair wheeled a red radio flyer wagon with butterfly decorations painted on it right by my door and stopped. Sitting in the wagon was a tiny little girl with a baldhead. She was wearing a little pink shirt and she was smiling. The man stayed outside my door, but started talking to me.

"Are you Charlie?" he asked.

"Yes, is she Hannah Grace?"

"Yep, this is Hannah Grace and I'm her dad, Jarrod. We were told that we needed to meet you." He turned to the small, smiling girl in the wagon. She almost shined to me, her presence felt warm and happy. "Say hi to Charlie." He instructed her. She waved and smiled shyly, then turned to look at her dad. She was the cutest thing I had ever seen.

"Hi Hannah Grace, I'm Charlie and this is my brother Blake." I pointed at my brother lying on his cot. She smiled and looked at her dad, she seemed so shy but so sweet.

"Okay Hannah Grace," her dad began to speak to her. "Blow Charlie kisses and I'll wheel you around some more." She put her hand to her mouth and started blowing me kisses as she was wheeled away. That small act made my day. What a beautiful little girl.

"Bye, Hannah Grace." I said. I was so glad to meet her, although I wished it were under better circumstances. Meeting her made me think even more about what I could do to help little children like her. There had to be something, anything.

Angela came back in and checked on my IVs. She shut my door as she left, but my mind was still on all of the other children that were in the oncology unit with me. I wanted to help them. I was having trouble falling asleep because I was thinking about my new little bald friend, Hannah Grace; I wished the medical staff and the researchers could cure her. I prayed for her and all of the other adolescents and children I had seen in the hospital. I wondered why those kids were the ones this happened to, but I knew I would never get that answer. The only conclusion I could come to before falling asleep was that there was something special about those small children. They're little bald angels, I thought, smiling as I closed my eyes.

I opened my eyes the next morning with an answer as to how I could help. My Uncle Perry had bought me a camera when I was still in PICU, and I was determined to film my entire experience with this cancer that had tried to take over my body, no matter how long it lasted. I had to tell my story anyway I could. I thought that maybe I could explain it in a way that somebody else my age or younger could understand. For the next two months, that camera would rarely be turned off. I wanted to create a documentary for other children and adolescents with AML to watch, so that they would know what to expect and that they weren't alone.

I also called my sister and asked that she bring me a journal that day when she came to visit. I wanted to get all of my thoughts written down. Even though I didn't talk much with my family about the possibility of death, I knew my chances. I had researched AML on my sister's laptop the first day I was in the hospital; I had a thirty percent chance of living out the next five years. In case I didn't make it, I wanted everyone to know how I felt and what I thought about my experience. I told my sister that I hoped to maybe have a memoir if I survived, but if I didn't I wanted her to write my story for me. She promised she would.

I wanted to do more than just tell my story, though. I wanted to do anything and everything to make a difference in the lives of other children and adolescents struggling with cancer. I wanted to start a foundation just for them. My foundation, the LiveLovely Foundation, was born that day. If even one person's life could be saved through my foundation, it would be worth starting it. This was another duty that I asked my sister to take care of for me if I were to go with out finishing it myself. She promised me this as well. Somehow I felt more peaceful knowing that no matter what happened, I was taking this experience and making something good come of it. Positive attitude leads to positive outcomes; I repeated that to myself everyday.

Give Thanks, Who Needs Hair Anyway?

Eventually, the inevitable happened. I woke up one morning with pieces of hair lying on my pillow. I ran my fingers through my hair and more fell out. I looked at my hands; they were covered in my hair. I had been dreading this moment since I had gotten my diagnosis. I didn't want to lose my hair, it made being a cancer patient official. I woke my brother up and we decided it was time to shave our heads. My sister had already cut twelve inches of her hair off in an effort to prepare me for my ordeal, and Blake had promised to shave his head the day I shaved mine. He promised to do everything he could to experience everything I would encounter right along beside me.

Blake turned on the electric razor and slowly began removing my hair with it. I cringed as I watched clumps of my hair fall in the hospital floor around my feet. I began to feel sick and closed my eyes until the ordeal was over. Once it was done, my brother shaved his own. I saw myself in the mirror with out hair for the first time and I was surprised to see that I didn't look too bad with a bald head. A little more like a cancer patient, but not bad.

I had been in the hospital for about three weeks. After my scary and tumultuous PICU stay and once my first round of chemo was finished, I felt more confident in myself and was relieved to have made such progress in my treatment. I felt less afraid of leukemia and more prepared to face whatever trials were to come. I felt relaxed in the hospital. I knew it would be a while before I started my second induction round of chemo. I had finally pieced the entire plan to save my life together and I felt I had a pretty good idea of what lie ahead.

I had responded really well to the first round of chemotherapy, which was three different medicines administered to me at different times through my central line. I received cytarabine (also known as Ara-C), daunorubicin, and etoposide. Well, the doctors had planned on giving me etoposide, but my parents found out that etopophos would be better for me because of the lower occurrence of reactions as compared to etoposide.

During the first round, which is known as first induction, I was given the chemotherapy drugs for ten days. The goal of induction chemotherapy is to bring the cancer into remission. Remission would be when my blood cell counts returned to normal and my bone marrow samples showed no sign of disease (less than five percent of cells are leukemia cells). To get to the goal of remission, all of my bone marrow was basically annihilated in hopes that as it would rehabilitate its self, it would no longer manufacture the leukemia cells. Because I didn't have any good white blood cells, I basically didn't have an immune system. So, after my first induction, I stayed in the hospital for almost a month because my immune system needed time to rebuild its self. Most of the time I was on steady antibiotics that were acting as my immune system. After my counts had come up (they were still extremely low, but up as far as my condition was concerned), I would start my second round of chemotherapy, which was called second induction. Second induction was supposed to take ten days as well. Nobody knew if I would go home before second induction or if I would still be at the hospital when it came time, it just depended on how well my body bounced back after the first induction. Once I finished both of these treatments, I would be reevaluated and the doctors and my parents would decide on the best way to finish my treatment. They had two choices depending on how my bone marrow looked: I could receive up to five more rounds of consolidation chemotherapy, or I could receive one more strong chemotherapy treatment and then have a bone marrow transplant.

Neither one of them sounded like anything I really wanted to do, but I knew I would have to do one of them. I assumed that it would probably be better not to get a bone marrow transplant. Although, I knew my family probably didn't want me to, I had already researched acute myeloid leukemia and found information on my odds and the usual symptoms after bone marrow transplants and chemotherapy. I knew how bad they both were, but I didn't really have a choice.

I had a better understanding of everything that was happening than most people thought, mainly because I didn't feel the need to dwell on it. I had developed the attitude that what was going to happen was going to happen and I just had to make the best of it along the way.

———

There was never a dull moment when I was at Children's. Once I started feeling good again, I loved getting out of my room and socializing with others in the hospital. My brother and I spent many nights after our family had left standing out by the nurse's station and chatting away with the nurses and other patients that had drifted out of their rooms. Once I even met a girl who was doing homework out at the nurse's station. Blake and I tried to help her, but even though she had asked for it, it seemed she didn't really need it. She solved most of the problems on her own.

Then there were times when Blake and I would stay up all night playing games on the computer. We were hooked up to headsets; so that we could talk to the people we were playing with. Many good quotes came from the guys on the other end of the headset at three in the morning. If Tab was spending the night, I would take my headphones off and turn the volume all the way up on the computer so that she could hear what the guys were saying too. She would just listen and laugh while me and Blake played.

Then, there were the times that I never expected to happen. Like the night me, my dad and my big brother and sister stayed up until the early morning hours crying and hoping to make up for lost time. I'll never forget that night because that was the night I realized the special connection I shared with my family, we all recognized that it wasn't something every family had and we had been very blessed to realize that.

It all started when my dad got upset about some of the pictures my sister had chosen to place on my bulletin board that was at that point hanging on the wall of room four forty-four. I watched for a short while as my dad lectured my sister on her selection of pictures and tears began to well in my sister's eyes. I calmly asked my brother if he could take my sister and step outside for a minute. Once they had left and shut the door behind them, I asked my dad to not be so hard on my sister and explained to him that doing things like decorating my room with that bulletin board were little ways that my sister could help take care of me and make me feel better when she felt so out of control. Just like Blake never left my side, that was his way to help me and make me feel better, they couldn't fight the disease for me, but they could use their own unique skills and interests to do whatever they could for me. I could see that my dad clearly understood and I even noticed some tears beginning to form in his eyes. I don't think I had ever seen my dad cry.

My brother and sister knocked on the door. "Y'all can come back in." I said. I noticed that Blake and Tab both had been crying. I had seen Blake cry several times since I had been in the hospital, but Tab was different. Tab rarely showed her emotions, and only did so when she had held them in so long they came out on their own. I guess Dad noticed they had been crying too, and apologized to my sister and to my brother as well. He had realized that he was trying to cope with what was happening by trying to control everything he could.

That night, we talked about things that I believe we would have never talked about if I hadn't been diagnosed with cancer.

Before my diagnosis my mom and my dad had separated. I always wanted to know what really happened between them, and that night, my dad finally answered that question. He also told Blake, Tab, and I about what he was like growing up and we heard stories about him that we'd never heard before. We all had our turns to talk, we told each other secrets and cried about things in our past that we couldn't change. Then we all made a covenant together; we would never take each other for granted again. My dad said, "We already made that mistake, and we won't make it again." We knew that we could never go back and change the past, but we also knew that we would never take each other for granted again.

Before I knew it, it was Thanksgiving. I couldn't believe that I had been in the hospital almost an entire month. Although I had been through a lot, time seemed to pass rather quickly in that hospital. At that point in my treatment, my family had basically begun living their lives for me. At first, this bothered me more than anything, I hated that I was holding everyone in my family back from living their normal lives, but I soon realized how much pleasure it brought them to help take care of me, and I thought, who am I to take that pleasure away from them? They were just as scared as I was, I could at least give them a chance to feel like they had made a difference in this fight for me.

My brother had made the decision to leave medical school for a year (which I knew was a big deal, even though he tried to convince me it wasn't), my sister had left her job and her life in Nashville behind shortly after I was diagnosed, and my dad rarely, if ever went further away from me than the short drive from the hospital to the hotel. My mother was already living her life for me before any of this ever happened, so she didn't really have to change much besides the forty-five minute commute from our home in Jasper to the hospital. Although Chandler had already missed many days of school, my sister and mother had decided to take turns staying with him in Jasper and making sure he got to school, just so he could still have some sense of normalcy. So, they had become accustomed to that commute.

Although I hated having cancer and I hated the huge change in mine and everyone in my family's life, I liked that all my family had to do in the world was be with each other and take care of each other. All other distractions had faded away. Our biggest issue to address was how we were going to have a big, traditional thanksgiving all together, while I was still in the hospital. My sister asked me what I wanted to do for Thanksgiving when she came to visit me on the Monday before Thanksgiving Thursday. I hadn't really thought about it until then, but apparently she had been struggling with how we would still have a real family Thanksgiving.

"I know that a bunch of families and past patients are bringing food on Thanksgiving for everyone up here to the parent's lounge." I told my sister.

"Well, you still want our regular Thanksgiving dinner, right? You know, Mom's dressing and pecan pie?"

"Oh, yeah. I definitely want Mom to cook and everything, but I guess we'll just have to figure out a way to do it in here." I pointed around four forty-four.

"Well, I've been thinking that maybe we could just have our family Thanksgiving on Wednesday. Then the parent's lounge would be available for just our family, right?"

"Yeah, do that!"

"Do you know if anybody else will be using the parent's lounge that day?"

"I'll call Catherine in real quick and ask her." I buzzed the red button that was sitting on the nightstand next to my bed, I heard it ring at the nurse's station, and then I heard Catherine talking in the background, "Catherine!" I yelled for her to come in my room. She came in smiling and joking around as usual.

"What can I help you with in here?"

"Listen, we want to have our family's Thanksgiving dinner on Wednesday in the parent's lounge. Is anybody else going to be using it on that day?"

"What time would you want to use it?" Catherine asked. My sister responded this time.

"I was thinking around three in the afternoon."

"I'll check and make sure, but I'm pretty sure you guys will be able to use it. I know no one else will be using the parent's lounge on Wednesday, except for the doctors after they do their rounds, but I'm sure they'll meet somewhere else so you guys can use it."

"Oh, we don't want to put anybody out." My sister started to respond, but I interrupted her and just asked Catherine to ask the doctors if they would mind if we used it. Catherine assured my sister that the doctors and residents had other places they could meet at, so it really wouldn't be a big deal. I felt that my sister was relieved now that Thanksgiving plans were falling into place. I was sad that we wouldn't be home, but Thanksgiving in the hospital wouldn't be so bad as long as I got my mom's home cooking.

Before I knew it, it was my family's Thanksgiving Day. My sister told me they would get to the hospital by three o'clock that afternoon, but it ended up being about an hour later than that. Blake and I were so excited about Thanksgiving that we decided to try and stay up all night until my family got there that afternoon. Unfortunately, I was given medicine at about noon that made me really tired. I woke up to my sister shaking my bed and calling my name. She apparently had been doing it for the last hour, but I had no idea.

"Char! Char, get up! Char! It's Thanksgiving! Get up! We got you some pecan pie!" She was yelling anything she could think of to get me to wake up. I could hear my dad telling her to just let me sleep and leave me alone.

"No!" she said, "He's been looking forward to this, and he's going to get up and enjoy it! He'll be much more upset if we let him sleep until the food gets cold!" I heard what she was saying and she was right. I was extremely exhausted, but I wanted to get up so badly. I finally mustered up enough energy to roll over and talk to my sister.

"I'm up. I'm up." I said groggily, trying to adjust my eyes to the room.

"Good! I brought you a plate of food; you can eat a little bit in here and then come to the parent's lounge. We have the whole table set up." My sister busily readied my little, rolling bedside table for me to eat with out having to get up out of the bed. I looked around and saw my brother and his girlfriend sitting on one of the cots in my room, Blake had a plate of food. Dad was on the other cot; he also had a plate of food. I thought about giving them a hard time for not waiting on me, but I was still so groggy and tired I didn't really want to do anything but eat the food my sister had brought me.

I noticed that my sister had given me very small portions of everything, even though she knew I liked to eat very large portions, especially on Thanksgiving. I realized that she had intended for me to eat just enough to want more so I would come to the parent's lounge. I barely ate what was on the plate my sister had brought me anyway because I wanted to go in the parent's lounge and visit with everyone while I ate. My sister stood and watched me.

"Alright guys, let's go to the parent's lounge." I said as I pushed my bedside table with the plate of food my sister had brought me on it away and sat up in my bed. My sister quickly grabbed clean clothes for me to change into from my closet. I put on the clothes she handed me and grabbed my toboggan, in case my bald head got cold. I turned around to pull the metal roller that my IV was attached to out so that I could push it down the hall with me since I was receiving medicine at the time. When I turned back around with my IV, I saw my sister standing in front of me with her arm extended. She was handing me a mask. Although I didn't want to wear it, and I did put up a small fight, I slipped it on to settle my sister's worried mind. My entire family had become increasingly protective and wouldn't let me go anywhere with out a mask on, protecting me from any harmful germs in the air. Once I had my mask on, we walked to the parent's lounge to eat with the rest of my family. I couldn't wait to see my littler brother, Chan.

The nurses all smiled and said their hellos as I walked down the hallway of the fourth floor, wheeling my IV beside me. My sister was telling me about all of the food they had brought and how many wagons it took them to roll it all up. I was still tired, but my excitement had given me a second wind. My sister opened the door of the parent's lounge for me. The smell of my mom's home cooking rolled out at me, I immediately felt warmth and happiness all around me. It was almost as good as being home. There was a long table in the middle of the room covered with white cloth. Every inch of the table was covered in containers of food, and it was all things that I loved, cooked specifically by my mother. My cousin, Alex, sat on a chair in the back of the room, my mother was sitting at a chair in the middle of the table, my sister's boyfriend sat at the far end of the table and Chan had run up next to me when I walked in to give me a hug. My dad, sister, Blake, and his girlfriend were all standing around me waiting for me to choose my seat. I pushed my IV in, and sat at the chair nearest to the door. Everyone else filled in the seats around me and our paper plates were soon piled high with all of the amazing dishes that Thanksgiving Day allows.

I dove into my food, savoring every bite, because I knew this year, since I was in the hospital, I wouldn't have any leftovers. I was so thankful that I was not getting chemo and all of the food tasted normal, with out that chemotherapy taste that I had so recently discovered. I ate my mom's turkey and dressing, mashed pota-toes, potato salad, peas, and continued eating until I had sampled almost every dish. Then my sister brought out dessert, she had brought a special ice cream cake for me and she had also made peanut butter and chocolate pie. My mom had already set out the pecan pie and pumpkin pie, I mostly ate pecan pie because it's always been my favorite, but I tried a little of everything. We smiled and laughed the whole time. The conversation was full and happy and never boring. I felt love and peace wash over me as I looked around the room at my family's smiling faces, and realized that the love we share is all that matters. I proudly announced to my family, "This is the best Thanksgiving I've ever had." I smiled from ear to ear. I looked at my mom and her eyes filled with tears, but she was smiling.

Hospital Release

In the beginning of December, I found out that I would be going home before my next round of chemotherapy from my nurse practitioner, Kensie. She had been on my case since my first day in the hospital; she was the person that always did my spinal taps. The more I got to know her, the more I liked her. She walked in my room smiling that day, proud to tell me that I would soon be at home in my own bed.

"Well, like how long? Because, I've heard that I would be going home soon a couple of times, but I haven't gone home yet." I responded to her, obviously lacking the enthusiasm she had expected.

"I'm very certain that you will be going home on December third, tomorrow, as long as you do well off of your antibiotics tonight. Your counts are looking good and you're looking good, so we thought we'd get you home before your next round starts." Kensie spoke as if I really wanted to go home, I liked the hospital and I loved my room.

"When do I start my next round? Isn't it really soon?" I questioned her.

"You're scheduled to start on Monday."

"That's only a few days at home. I might as well just stay here through my second round. It'll be easiest, and I don't really mind to stay."

Kensie laughed and said, "It really will be best for you to go home for a few days. You need to get a little bit of normalcy in your life. I'm glad you like it here, we like having you here, but you've got to go home."

"We'll just see about that, Kensie." I said in a joking way to her, knowing that I would be going home before my second round began.

She looked at my brother and sister who were sitting on one of the cots together and said; "I don't think I've ever had to kick a kid out of a hospital room before." We all laughed, but for some reason I seriously wanted to stay in the hospital. Maybe I was just scared that going back to the place I had lived in for so long with out cancer would make me realize how drastically my life had changed. I hadn't been back there since I was diagnosed; the hospital had become my "cancer" home. I guess somewhere inside, I had hoped that when I went home, I would go home like I always had, with out cancer, but that wasn't the case.

As Kensie prepared to leave, Blake stopped her and asked, "Have the results of his test come back yet? Do we know for certain what his subtype is?"

"Oh yeah!" Kensie said, "Let me go get them for you."

I was surprised that she said yes. Blake had asked that same question almost every time Kensie or one of my doctors came in my room. I really didn't want to know my subtype or what my "chances" were. I felt apprehensive as Kensie was going to retrieve my results. She hurried back in my room and handed Blake a folded up piece of paper. She assured us that she would be back later, and she was gone. I watched Blake unfold the paper, and read the results to himself as we all sat in silence. I could tell that he was scared, disappointed, and a little confused just by the expression he wore on his face. I looked at Tab and I knew she saw it too.

"What does it say, Blake?" Tab asked, Blake responded with silence. Tab prodded with the same question again. Blake looked up with anger in his eyes and said, "Tab, I don't know. Don't worry about it. Take Charlie down to get his x-ray done."

She wore a stone expression and responded with only, "Fine."

She walked out of the room and wheeled a wheel chair in for me. "Come on, Char." She said.

"You're going to go get me some food after this right?" I asked, eager to change the subject.

"Yeah, I know you're starving, you've been NPO since midnight, right?"

"Actually, two this morning, but I am starving." She started to wheel me down the hall. I was glad to be getting this x-ray over with. I hated being NPO. When I was NPO, it meant that I couldn't eat after a certain time. Because I was to get an x-ray today, I hadn't been allowed to eat until it was over.

We made it down the elevator and through the hall of the second floor to the x-ray room. We had to wait outside because there was another patient in the room. My sister and I stood in silence; I knew what she was thinking about and then she said, "I just wish I knew what that paper said."

I responded to her by talking about what kind of food I wanted her to get for me once the x-ray was over. I guess she realized that I didn't want to talk about it, and she quickly changed gears for the new conversation. Soon, the door opened and a girl was wheeled out, she never even noticed that my sister and I stood next to her as she was wheeled by. She stared straight ahead with a blank stare; I wondered what was wrong with her.

My sister wheeled me into the room and put on one of the aprons supplied by the hospital that said "mom" so that she could stay in the room with me while I got my x-rays. A technician came in and helped me get positioned on the table. As my stomach and chest were scanned, I laid and stared straight ahead. I tried to focus on one tile on the ceiling, but the way the machine moved me back and forth and jerked every time it stopped, threw my focus off. I tried not to think about what that little piece of paper Kensie had given my brother said.

The next morning my parents arrived at my beautiful "cancer" home, room four forty-four, and prepared to start packing it up. I felt very attached to my room and I was having a hard time going home, but I sucked it up for everyone else. Before my parents began packing, the nurses gave a crash course on my in-home care. She gave them instructions on how to take care of my central line and when to give me all the different medicines I had been prescribed. They also warned my parents that if I were to ever spike a fever, I had to be brought to the hospital immediately. I was taken off of my IV, and prepared for the ride home.

My brother and I waited outside my door as my parents wheeled wagon after wagon of my belongings out of room four forty-four. I watched each small possession pass me in those little red wagons as I sat in my wheel chair wearing a mask. My brother stood behind me with his hand resting on the back of my chair. Finally, the last wagons were filled and it was time to go home. Just as they had done the day I was wheeled to room four forty-four after my stay in PICU, the nurses all stood and applauded as I was wheeled down the fourth floor hallway and to the elevator with my family in tow. I was opening a new chapter in the journey of my fight. For the first time since diagnosis, I would be at home. Uncertainty promoted fear, but I couldn't hold myself back. I had to take the next step, and I prayed that it would turn out positively.

Welcome Home

My homecoming wasn't quite how I thought it would be. Everyone seemed ecstatic to have me home, and in a way I was happy to be home too. But I knew the adjustments I was about to have to make were going to make everything that I had just experienced and what I knew I faced in the future much more real, and I was scared I wasn't prepared for that.

I got out of my mom's car and looked up at the house I had grown up in. The white, vinyl siding stopped just under the window of the room that had always been my playroom, beneath it were three garage doors. I can never remember a time I came home and didn't open that middle garage door with the remote that hung on my mother's overhead mirror and walked into our house through the all glass door in our garage. This small, unnoticed ritual was now totally different. Everything else had stayed the same, but I had changed. Although I walked through our middle garage and opened the same glass door I had opened for as long as I could remember, it was almost as strange as walking in to a different house or through a different door. I was different now, my house was the same, but now I had cancer.

The first thing I noticed when I walked into the house was the strong smell of alcohol and cleaner. My mother and sister had been diligently cleaning and sanitizing every inch of our home for the past few weeks. I was a little disturbed that it didn't smell like the home I had grown to love and cherish. My beloved home now smelled like a hospital because of my weak immune system. My sister and my cousin were inside waiting to greet me. They patted my back and smiled, glad to have me home. My mom and dad walked in behind me carrying my bags, Blake followed behind them. I walked around the house, remembering the way things used to be, before I got cancer. I opened the door to the master bedroom that my parents had always slept in. Now, this room was mine. It looked completely different than I had ever seen it. A king sized bed sat against one of the walls, it was facing a large, flat screen TV. There was a small stand beside the bed with a lamp on it. Windows that were covered by thick, tan curtains covered one of the walls. There was a small cot made up next to the bed I would be sleeping in. The room was bare, no pictures on the wall, it looked nothing like I remembered it.

I walked into the bathroom that was attached to the master bedroom. Everything was stripped clean. The floors shined, it was immaculate. On the long bar that had a sink on either side of it that was to my left as I walked in the bathroom were boxes of medical paraphernalia. I saw stacks of gauze, a couple boxes of masks, a box of alcohol swabs, and different medicines. I was out of the hospital, but now my home had been turned into a make-shift hospital. I became overwhelmed and decided I needed to leave my old home and my new hospital for a while.

I walked back into the family area and my sister was grabbing her car keys, she was leaving to pick Chandler up from school. I asked her if I could drive. She responded with an excited, "Yeah!" And hurried about grabbing alcohol wipes. She ran ahead of me to give her car a quick, but very thorough wipe down. She even wiped off her keys before handing them to me. It felt good to finally feel a little in control. My mom forced a mask into my hand as I walked out the door; I slid it into my pocket once I was out of her sight and was glad that Tab never told me to put it on. My sister and I turned up the radio and sang loudly in between our small talk. I felt normal and free as I turned the wheel and started down the windy back roads of our little town. I was excited when I pulled in to the horseshoe shaped driveway in front of Chandler's school and joined the long line of other vehicles waiting on young and rowdy children to hop inside. Chandler had no idea that I had been released from the hospital that day and I was eager to see his reaction when he saw who was picking him up.

The line of cars in front of the elementary school stretched as far down the road as I could see. Luckily, I had pulled in just before the after school rush and was positioned at the front of the line of cars. It was strange for me to be doing something so normal. For over thirty days I had not stepped one foot out of Children's Hospital, and now here I was in line at my little brother's school with all of the other older siblings and parents. It was a little like someone had dashed cold water on my face. The world didn't stop when I was diagnosed with leukemia. Everyone else continued on their same track of life with nothing changed, but somehow it was hard for me to believe that my life had changed so incredibly and everyone else's remained the same.

I heard the school bell ring through the windows of the car and my sister and I watched the seas of smiling, young faces pouring out of every door of the school. They were all lead by their teachers who seemed just as relieved and excited that the school day was over as the children were. I scanned every face and small backpack trying to spot Chandler. I watched a group of children that looked to be Chandler's age, taking their seats on the benches under the awning adjacent from where my sister and I were sitting in my sister's car. I finally spotted him, and he obviously had no clue we were there. I watched as he smiled and giggled with his friends, all of them wearing whatever food they had for lunch that day on their faces and clothes. They were a funny group to look at. My sister rolled her window down and waved Chandler over to where we were. His eyes lit up when he saw her and he came running over to the car.

One of the children on the safety patrol at Chandler's school opened the back door for Chandler. He threw his backpack in and prepared his skinny body to jump in as well, but then he saw me. I couldn't do justice in trying to describe the look of joy and happiness that shined all over his face, it made me feel proud, complete, whole, and happy too. He turned to his friends that were still sitting on the bench he had just left and yelled, "Oh yeah! Score one for my brother back home!" He then jumped in the car with a permanent smile plastered across his face.

───────────────

Picking up Chandler was one of my favorite memories of coming home. I knew how much he needed me, and I was glad to be home for him, but when my two siblings and I arrived back home it was time for me to finally face the reality of my new life. When earlier confronted with it, I had found a way to escape, but now I knew I had to come to terms with this new reality.

The house was relatively quiet and everyone had busied themselves with various tasks around the house. This provided me with the perfect opportunity to be alone for a moment, something I hadn't done since I had been diagnosed. I walked into my new bedroom and shut the door behind me. I took everything in, the smells, the way it looked, how the air felt around me. I touched the TV that had been in my playroom for so long. I walked around the room and stared at the blank walls that once had portraits of angels hanging on them. I felt stripped down, bare, like everything in my life had been taken away. I missed my old life, all I wanted was to have it back and I knew I never would. I slid down the wall as I finally broke down in the overwhelming circumstances surrounding me. My tears ran down my cheeks and I held my head in my hands. I finally let everything flow; the fear, the sadness, and the confusion. I just cried, and soaked in the glory of the release it gave me.

My mother came in to check on me shortly after I started my tear shedding. Like any mother would, she ran to me, but she couldn't hold me. She asked me what was wrong as she hurriedly tried to sanitize herself in hopes that if she would, she could hug me and make me feel better. I didn't want her to see me cry, I didn't want anyone to see me cry. I felt bad enough dealing with my circumstances and I couldn't stand to think about the fact that what was happening to me was hurting everyone else too. I know it hurt my mom to see me cry, so I asked her to leave. She begged me to let her stay and help me feel better, but all I really wanted to do was be alone. I got into my bed under all of my sterilized sheets and blankets and cried myself to sleep; in an odd way I never felt bad about that day, I was glad to have given myself the relief brought by the sweet release of those tears. It was like once I had cried my eyes dry, the Lord wiped the tears away for good and I was satisfied in my faith. All of that by just letting myself cry.

Blake shaved my head when I started loosing my hair

(Blake also shaved his head and Tab donated 10 inches of hers to Locks of Love)

Goodbye Old Life, Hello Cancer Life

The lyrics to one of my favorite songs from one of the newest hip hop artists blasting from my cell phone woke me up a few hours after I had dosed off from my crying spell. I reached over to the small nightstand next to my bed where I had laid my phone to charge. The small letters on the screen read "Eddie." Eddie was my best friend. We lived next door to each other since I was three years old. Eddie has been around for as long as I can remember. Over the years, our friendship had evolved into a true brotherhood. I felt a stirring of excitement when I realized that now that I was home, I could spend time with Eddie doing some of the things we used to do. I clicked the little green button on my phone and answered.

"Hello." I said.

"Charlie?" I heard Eddie's confused response; I must've sounded sick since I had just woken up. I cleared my throat a little and tried to make my voice sound as spritely as possible.

"Yeah."

"Are you home now?"

"Yeah, I'm laying in bed."

"I'll be over in like thirty seconds." He said quickly, and hung up the phone. I smiled to myself. Eddie's call was what I needed to lift my spirits after the shock of coming back home. I decided that even though cancer had caused me to have a "new" life, I could make it just as good as my "old" life, although it would be different, it could still be good.

I was still lying in bed when I heard the doorbell ring. I heard my Mom greeting Eddie, so I rolled over and turned the light on that was next to my bed. My mom knocked on the door and after hearing my usual, "come in," response lead Eddie in. My mom had set up a sterilization station outside of my bedroom. There was a sign that instructed anyone entering my room to scrub their hands all the way up to their elbows thoroughly with Clorox wipes and hand sanitizer. When Eddie walked in, he was still rubbing the hand sanitizer in. Mom left Eddie and I alone so she could go back to the laundry room to continue cleaning all of my clothes she had brought back from the hospital.

Eddie and I talked to each other pretty much every day, and he was a frequent visitor of mine in the hospital. So, we had been sitting around talking to each other for over thirty days because we couldn't do anything else. I longed to get back to going out around town and seeing friends. I wanted to get out and experience the world; I wanted to actually live. I had been a captive of the hospital for so long, now that I had the chance, I wanted to run and breath the fresh air outside. I told Eddie that I wanted to get out, but I knew it would be difficult to convince my parents that it would be okay. Because my immune system was so weak, they had already gone overboard with taking precautions. I couldn't imagine that they would let me out into the public with all of the germs I could possibly pick up. We tried to occupy ourselves for a while, chatting and playing on the internet, but the itch to get out was too strong. I called my mom into my room and asked her the question that she had to assume was coming.

"Can I go out with Eddie?" I asked.

"Where do you want to go?" She responded with a concerned look.

"We can just go get some food, Eddie will sanitize his car, and I won't get out." I responded.

"Tim!" She yelled at my dad.

He yelled, "What?" As he came walking towards the room.

"Charlie wants to go get some food with Eddie. Eddie sanitized his truck and Charlie's not going to get out." She said, obviously on my side, and hopeful that it would be safe enough for me to spend time with friends like a "normal" teenager.

I could see that Dad was rolling the thought around in his head. I watched him weigh the risks of my small adventure, and then he said, "I guess that will be alright as long as Charlie wears a mask."

"Yes!" I shouted gleefully as I jumped up out of bed.

"Eddie, let me help you go wipe your truck down a little bit before Charlie gets in." My dad said, obviously worried. Eddie grabbed a box of Clorox wipes and hurried out the door behind my dad. I went in my bathroom and washed my hands and face. I pulled a new toothbrush out of the bag on my sink. Since I started chemo, I wasn't allowed to reuse toothbrushes and the hospital had given me some little pink sponge toothbrushes that were less abrasive on my mouth than a regular toothbrush. I still used a regular toothbrush, though, I just felt like my teeth didn't get clean enough with the hospital toothbrushes. Fortunately, I had so far not gotten a bad case of mouth and throat sores that come as a side effect from some of the chemotherapy I was given. So, I decided I would use a regular toothbrush for as long as I could stand it. I gave my teeth a slow, gentle rub and rinsed my mouth out. I went in my closet and looked over all the clothes, deciding which shirt I would most like to wear. For a moment, I talked some sense into myself, asking myself why I was so busy getting ready, I wouldn't even be getting out of the car, but I brushed that off. I didn't want to ruin this most perfectly "normal" adventure I was about to have.

When I had changed, I grabbed a small, Mickey Mouse mask out of the box on my sink and shoved it into my pocket. I sat by our glass garage door in one of the chairs that I had pulled away from our dining room table as I slid on my shoes and watched my dad and Eddie scrubbing the inside of Eddie's truck with those bleach wipes my mom loved. I had the excitement of a little kid on Christmas, I felt like I couldn't get my shoes on fast enough. I walked out to where they were and when my dad saw me he picked up all of the wipes he had used and took them to the garbage can, he then grabbed the box of sanitizing equipment and told me to have a good time as he hurried inside. Eddie and I watched my dad walk inside and disappear into the light of my house. Eddie looked at me and smiled as he wiped the keys to his truck with a sanitizing wipe, "You drive." He said, as he tossed his keys to me. I grabbed them and grinned. I had wanted to drive Eddie's truck ever since he got it, and now I was finally getting the chance. He stood next to the driver's side door as I climbed in. Eddie shut the door and walked around to his side. I started the truck and put my hands on the steering wheel, I couldn't erase my smile as I listened to the sound of the engine and felt the vibrations on my seat. Eddie climbed in and looked at me, "Let's go." I said as we pulled out of my driveway. I was free.

When I made it back to my house a few hours later, it was obvious that my family had been very busy since I had been gone. I walked into my room that had been bare when I left, now, there were posters hanging on my walls. I looked at what when I had left had been a bare room, and now as I glanced around it still looked bare in ways, but it had a younger feel. The headboard of the large bed that had once been my parents but now was mine was sitting on the wall to the left of where I stood in the doorway. The small nightstand was still sitting next to it, but had been decorated with the hospital supplies that I had to use most frequently through out the day and night. On the wall to the right of the bed hung the NBA poster that had been hanging in my hospital room. Over the bed hung two more posters that had also been hanging in home sweet home, room four forty-four at the hospital.

As I walked further into the room, I examined the two small chairs that had once been sitting in my playroom. They were black, leather chairs that sat on the floor and had speakers on either side of the headrests; my brothers and I had used them to play our video games in for years. Now these two chairs were sitting directly in front of my TV and all of my game systems were hooked up. On the wall next to the TV hung yet another poster that had been in my hospital room. As I requested, the things I had left laying on my floor, like cards and gifts I had received in the hospital, were still essentially untouched and in the same place I had left them. I wanted to go through them again before I put them away. For some reason this kind gesture from my family did not make me as happy or more comfortable as they probably expected it would. I was devastated.

I didn't want my family to know that somehow the gift they had tried to give me had actually done the opposite of what they had hoped. I looked back and saw Eddie talking to my mom; I walked all the way into the room alone and shut my door. I sat down on the right side of my bed. I stared up at the collage of pictures my sister had made me, once hanging in my hospital room, now hanging in my room at home. I scanned over pictures of my family and I at Disney World. One picture in particular stood out, Chandler and I on the teacups in Disney World. We were both looking over our shoulders at the camera and smiling. The vivid colors intermixed with the carefree, happy expressions on our faces made it the perfect picture to frame. I wish I could feel that carefree and happy again. I questioned myself and my emotions about the room makeover provided by my family, but I knew why I was upset. I asked that nothing in the room be changed or touched. I felt so out of control, nothing I wanted mattered, I was just supposed to know that whatever decisions were made for me by my doctors or my family were "what's best for me." It didn't feel that way.

I never questioned why this happened to me. I never asked why I got cancer. I was glad it was me; I don't think I could handle watching one of my family members suffer with a sickness like this. The one thing about my cancer that affected me most besides the way it affected my family was how out of control of my life felt since I was diagnosed. It didn't matter whether or not I wanted to have treatment or surgery; I had to do it if I wanted a chance to live. At the same time, I was no longer able to plan for my future. I didn't know if the treatment would work or not, how could I plan what would happen in a few years if I couldn't plan what would happen in a few days or weeks? I felt that my dreams had been stripped away, and now all that mattered was holding on to my family and hoping for more time to spend with them here on earth. I had come to terms with the loss sense of control involving the fate of my family by making myself feel like I was fighting to win the right to spend more time with my family. I had finally realized that I was never in control to begin with, I just felt like I was. No one is promised tomorrow. I had finally handed everything in the largest sense of my life over to the Great Physician.

However, I still wanted to be able to have a little say so in small, every day life. I wanted to be in control over how my room was decorated and who came in and out, and I felt that that had been taken away from me. I never said anything to my family about the decorating of my room, and they didn't mention it to me. I understood that all they wanted was to make me comfortable and happy, and they understood that I was experiencing some changes that were difficult to deal with. I took a few deep breaths and smiled. Even if I didn't feel like smiling, I would smile, and the longer I smiled, the more I wanted to keep on smiling. I opened the door of my new room and joined my family and Eddie to eat the dinner Eddie and I had just picked up.

Soon, all of my siblings, my dad, myself and Eddie all ended up with plates of seconds and drinks in my room. The TV was turned on to a movie my mom had bought for me as a coming home gift. We didn't really watch the movie, though; we sat around talking and laughing with each other as we had started to do more often since I had gotten sick. I was thankful for every memory I was able to make with my family, no matter how small it may seem. At one point my siblings and I began asking each other whom their favorite sibling was. I asked my sister and she thought seriously about who she would say, you could tell that she was having a hard time making her decision for favorite brother. As she thought, Chandler got impatient and everyone could tell. My sister asked him, "Who's your favorite sibling, Chandler?"

"Char!" He shouted matter-of-factly. We all laughed at the way he said it so seriously, like it was the obvious answer. When he noticed we were laughing, he responded by almost shouting, "Char should be everyone's favorite! For real! He's so awesome." We all laughed at that and everyone agreed with Chandler that I was their favorite. I felt so happy, and for a while, we all let my sickness slip our minds. When I realized that I had forgotten my situation, for a moment that I had let all worries about my cancer go, I looked around the room at everyone else and noticed how losing those worries, even just for a moment had an affect on everyone, not just me. The room was obviously lifted and everything felt lighter somehow. The carefree smiles of my family showed that they had allowed their weary minds to rest from the stress of worry, even if it was for just a moment. Moments like this are what I tried to fill my memories of this time in my life with.

Me and my best girl friends, Ju Ju (Julianna), Reegan, and Caro (Caroline).

Second Round

I hadn't been home for long, only a short few days, when it was time for me to go back to the hospital and start another ten day round of chemo. My family packed everything I would need for what we were hoping would be a short stay in the hospital. I had my computer and book of DVDs and a duffle bag with clothing and hygiene products. My brother had about the same amount of things. The drive to Birmingham had become so normal to my family, but this was only my second trip there. I felt the way I used to feel when I would go back to school after I had been out sick for a few days. I didn't mind going, although there were other things I would rather do, and we always arrived much more quickly than I thought we would.

This time, going to the hospital was much different than I remembered the first time being. My family and I walked in with a purpose; we knew where we had to be and what we were about to go through. The last time I walked through those doors, I had no idea what was about to happen and how my life would change. We walked into what the hospital called clinic. Clinic was a place where patients that were coming to the hospital regularly to receive treatments went to first. In clinic, a staff of doctors and nurses would check your vitals, possibly give you some medication and check your overall physical condition. Once they had all of their results in, they would make a decision on where to place you to receive the rest of your treatment. This was the first time I had been to clinic, but Sarah had been there before and she explained to me what it was like. I turned a corner on the second floor and walked into a room painted in bright colors with large, colorful pictures hanging on the wall. Rows of chairs filled almost the entire room; they all faced a glass window that had one single door beside it. My mom walked beside me as we approached the glass window and got checked in.

We waited only for a short moment and were soon called back into clinic by a young nurse. My parents and my big brother walked behind me as I followed the nurse down a long, narrow hallway. Small rooms were on either side of me. Eventually the hallway opened up to a large round nurses station across from a large room with a row of eight large leather chairs on either side. The nurse led me into that room and sat me in one of the chairs. My family settled themselves in other chairs and stools they could pull close to me. I looked around and noticed that there were a couple of other children also seated in this room full of black leather chairs. All of the chairs had a small, blue curtain that could be pulled fully closed for as much privacy as possible, they were kind of like tiny little rooms. Sterile hospital tables with numerous supplies and tools sat next to each chair. The other children climbed over the seats and jumped up and down, neither was older than seven and they both seemed energetic and healthy. My parents talked to one of the children's mother, her three year-old son, Jonah, was receiving chemotherapy for leukemia as well. He was just finishing his second round of chemotherapy, which is usually known as the most difficult round of therapy. Besides his bald head, you would never guess that he was sick at all. It amazes me how quickly young bodies can recover from almost anything. I smiled at Jonah, I felt a strong connection to him, we were both soldiers fighting the same battle.

My brother and my dad talked to me about what to expect when the doctors came out as my mom continued talking with Jonah's mother. I didn't really care to try and figure out what to expect anymore. I knew how quickly everything could change. My team of doctors walked into the large room I was sitting in, this time my head doctor was replaced by another female doctor that was oddly similar to my old doctor, Dr. Handler. They drew blood and checked my bone marrow to be sure that I was well enough to start my second round of chemotherapy. The last time they had checked my bone marrow was a few days before I left the hospital after my induction round of chemotherapy. I'll never forget hearing the results of my bone marrow tests. My mom and all of my siblings and I were down in the Children's Harbor playing basketball together. Dad came in the door and grabbed a ball that wasn't being used and he started shooting along with us. We all knew that he had been meeting with the doctors and that they would know if the chemotherapy was working depending on how my bone marrow looked. We all stopped and looked at him, "Well?" my sister prodded him.

"What?" he said.

"Seriously, Dad, what did the doctors say?" You could hear the fear and worry in my sister's voice.

"They said it looks great. Charlie's bone marrow looks like re-mission bone marrow." He announced to all of us smiling.

"Yes!" My sister shouted. We all celebrated the great news. I felt like I had accomplished something great. My dad decided he wanted to play a one on one game with me, which we hadn't done since I had been diagnosed. He was excited about this great, shining piece of hope that we had just received.

"Alright, just remember, go easy on me, I do have cancer." I said smiling.

"Nope, I'm playing you for real, you're in remission!" He dribbled around me as I laughed at him.

This time when the doctors returned with the results from my bone marrow tests, we did not celebrate. I was more nervous than

I thought I would be this time. Mostly, this was because I was trusting an almost entirely new medical team with my life. All of the doctors and residents were new, except one, he had been on my case when Dr. Handler was in charge. Formally, he was known as Dr. Arnold, but I just called him by his last name, Arnold.

It always takes a while to get used to and trust new caregivers. I felt comfortable with Arnold. Once, during my first stay in the hospital, he came in by himself to check on me. Because I was receiving chemotherapy injections in my spinal cord and the medical staff had to regularly give me spinal taps and draw out spinal fluid, I suffered from severely painful headaches. These headaches were caused by the lack of spinal fluid going up to my brain and balancing out the pressure on the membrane at the base of my skull that separates the spinal fluid from the fluid in which the brain floats. To prevent these headaches from occurring, I was instructed to lay completely flat for around thirty minutes to an hour after receiving spinal taps so that the rest of my spinal fluid that wasn't pulled out by a needle would be able to spread up to my brain easier, However, these headaches still occurred depending on how I was sleeping or if I coughed to hard. During one of my spells with these headaches, I had flipped myself around in my hospital bed. My head was lying where my feet would usually be and my feet were where my head would usually be. I had no pillow and was lying in only my underwear on top of my blankets. Arnold came into my room after I had finally managed to fall asleep, he had heard about my headache. He tiptoed in and stood over my head. I heard him click a pen and I opened my eyes. "What's up, Arnold." I said, nonchalantly. I had long before that incident let go of inhibitions about my body being seen or studied; there is no privacy when you're in the hospital with an acute cancer. Arnold laughed at my nonchalant response, and from that moment on, we became like friends. I liked Arnold.

However, when Arnold stood in front of me with the other doctors and announced what they had found and how my treatment plan was to change, I didn't know how to feel. I realized that he was a physician; he had to keep his emotions from interfering with his work. He couldn't be my friend that day; he had to be my doctor. He explained to my family in a calm, unrelated way, that my bone marrow did not look as good as they would like it to. It was having trouble re-building itself and the medical team on my case was concerned that because of my subtype (I only knew that my subtype was called Trisomy 8, Blake had eventually revealed the ugly truth to me, my survival rates were average at best) with out a bone marrow transplant, my treatment would not be successful. My medical team had expected my bone marrow to have improved much more than what it had, my platelets and white blood cell counts were low. Dr. Arnold explained that the team had decided to give me two more days to recover before I started second induction chemotherapy.

He also told us that he wanted to give me blood as soon as possible and was sure that some would be available for me by the next morning. I was happy and forgot about the bad news he had just given us when he said that he wanted to give me blood. Blood was a special commodity in the hospital. The medical staff had to ration out the blood that the patients received, you could only have blood if you really needed it, and of course, if they even had any. I never realized how short of a supply of blood there was, until I was diagnosed with cancer. Once I had gone through chemotherapy, I was regularly given blood, platelets, and plasma through an IV to keep me well. I often had to wait for long periods of time before ever getting any once the doctors had directed for me to receive some. Every time I received any of these special commodities, I felt great. Usually for at least the next couple of days after receiving blood products I felt totally healthy. There were times that I felt so bad that I would beg the medical staff for blood to make me feel better.

Arnold soon busted my excitement about receiving blood when he continued to talk to my family about bone marrow transplants. I heard him mention trisomy 8, which was rare and hard to treat. I didn't know the exact medical definition of trisomy 8, but I knew that it was associated with my cancer and that it was not as favorable as all the doctors on my case and my family had hoped my subtype would be. The thought of having a bone marrow transplant was extremely scary to me; I knew what the side effects and statistics were. I knew that I would feel like I had the flu for weeks afterwards and that my chances of survival were about thirty percent. I did not want to die the painful death that I knew a bone marrow transplant could cause. I also knew what Dr. Arnold was saying; a bone marrow transplant had now become my only shot. I prayed that I would somehow evade a bone marrow transplant and be cured through chemotherapy only, but it seemed that the answer to that prayer was no. When Dr. Arnold was finished briefing my family and I on my new treatment plans, the herd of doctors shuffled back down the hallway and out of sight. My brother looked at me and said, "Do you understand what Arnold was saying?"

"I need a bone marrow transplant." I said.

"Right, so now what we're looking at is…" He started to explain the situation to me, and I cut him off and said, "I don't want to know anymore, don't tell me anything else unless I ask." I knew enough already, I didn't want to flood my head with anymore medical jargon and statistics, instead I chose to just hope for the best and pray hard.

———————————————

The next day, I convinced my parents to let my brother and I go to clinic and get my blood alone. I loved having my parents around, but I really just needed my brother to be there. I worried about my parents and didn't want them to be concerned, I could talk to Blake about just about anything and I knew that he would shine a positive light on me and everything around me. The bond between the siblings in my family has always been very special and very strong. We watched out for each other and took care of one another. We had no secrets, nothing to hide. True love, the love between my siblings and I. Going to the hospital and staying at the hospital with Blake felt more like fun than anything else. I was happy and excited and so was Blake, we both knew how great I would feel after I received my blood that day.

Blake and I walked into clinic on time that morning and we didn't wait in the waiting room at all; the nurse immediately walked us back and sat us in the same large room with black leather chairs that we had been in yesterday. She told us to wait a few moments for the doctors to come in. Sarah was in clinic that day too and I had noticed her getting treatment on the other side of the room. Her area was now sectioned off, but we were texting each other as Blake and I waited for my blood. We waited for about thirty minutes and the doctors came out and talked to us. They informed us that they were still waiting on the blood product and that I would receive it as soon as it came in. We waited in the hospital for my blood that day for almost three hours, eventually we were told that they didn't have any blood for me that day and that we would have to come back to clinic tomorrow at the same time to receive blood. We were more than disappointed, but knew that it was always a possibility that blood wouldn't be available. We went home, tired and weary and once we were home, we slept until we woke up to go back to the hospital the next day.

I was feeling more rested that next morning, but still knew that I would feel much better once I had received blood. My brother and I traveled alone again to the hospital. When we arrived, we went through the same routine we had been through the previous two days. The nurse took us back to the room with the leather chairs and we sat and waited. The doctors came in and met with us and then left, and we waited some more. Eventually, we had waited for almost two hours. The nurse came out and explained to us that there was no blood again today and that I would have to wait until I came and checked in for my second induction chemotherapy the next day before any blood would be available for me. I couldn't believe it, my spirits were lowered. Hopefully, I would be able to get blood before I started chemotherapy the next day. I had been told several times by my family and my doctors that the second induction round of chemotherapy would be the most difficult I would have to go through. I believed the reason for that, for the most part, was the extremely weakened state that my body would already be in from the first induction I received only a few weeks earlier. I was hoping that if I could receive the blood before my chemo, it would make me stronger so I could get through this second round. My brother and I traveled the forty-five minutes back home, tired and disappointed.

As I lay in the bed that night and watched my mom, dad and older brother and sister prepare me to go back to the hospital for my second round, I could sense their nervousness and fear. We had all been worried about this round; we knew it was going to be a tough mountain to climb. I joked with them to relieve their tension, "See, I tried to tell everybody to just let me stay in the hospital. If everyone would've let me stay, I would be feeling really good because I would have some blood and you guys wouldn't have to be doing all of this packing and worrying." I smiled at them when they all stopped what they were doing to look at me and when they saw my smile, we all started to laugh. I understood why they were nervous, I was nervous too, but I had peace inside that told me everything would be okay.

When my mom, dad, brother and I arrived at the hospital the next afternoon, we reported to clinic first. The usual nurse came out and walked us down the hallway to the big room with leather chairs that I had spent the previous three mornings in. My medical team came out to talk with my family and I as they usually did and they told us that I would finally receive blood that day in clinic before I was checked into the hospital. My doctor went to review my latest bone marrow biopsy to determine if my body could handle chemotherapy. They had sent me home because my counts were too low last time, so I was anxious for what would happen this time. While the doctors were gone, a kind nurse that I had not yet met, came out and hooked me up to an IV to receive my blood while the doctors reviewed my case. I sat in my black leather chair with my family around me with a smile on my face as I finally got my blood products.

It was close to Christmas time and people dressed up as elves and Santa Clause came around with bags of toys and goodies for all of the kids sitting in the room with big leather chairs where I was. I'm sure they would go all over the hospital visiting children that day, but they treated each kid as special as the next. Sometimes, though, I could see the sadness in their eyes when they looked at me and in turn, I felt sad. I didn't want anyone to feel sorry for me. Most of the time though, I enjoyed meeting all of the people that came to bring cheer to the hospital. One of my favorite memories in the hospital is from this day. When the holiday visitors were making their rounds, a small group from a local church walked in. The group was mostly young kids, it looked like they had all tried to wear Christmas colors, but the clothes they wore were modest, at best. My brother and I looked at each other as they walked in, we were both not sure what to expect from this interesting group of people. As Santa and his helpers made their way down the hallway and out the doors to travel the rest of the hospital making visits, this group of kids huddled together in a small square in the center of the room. They stood for a moment with their heads staring down at the floor. I looked around the room, but didn't see a supervisor or a group leader. Others in the room were watching, including Sarah, who was also getting blood that day. Sarah texted me and expressed her curiosity about the group. As I was about to text her back, a beautiful sound came out of that group of huddled together kids. Everyone in the room stopped what they were doing and watched. The longer they sang, the stronger and more beautiful the sound they emitted became. They sang the most beautiful rendition of the Carol of the Bells that I had ever heard. I was astonished and I turned to look at my brother. His eyes were wide and his jaw was dragging on the floor. His face clearly showed that he was just as surprised as I was. They sounded beautiful. I texted Sarah and said, "Wow, I guess that's a lesson on never judging a book by its cover. Those kids are awesome."

When the kids were finished singing everyone clapped and those that could stand, did. It was moving and I couldn't help but feel like God had sent those kids there to help bring peace to our worried minds through their simple and glorious music. The tears of relief in the eyes of the mothers in that room showed that I was not only one that felt the glory of God in those kids that day. Soon after the kids finished singing and began their walk down the hallway to sing to another group of kids, my medical staff led this time by Dr. Arnold approached my family and I. We were both happy and scared when he said that my counts were a little better, and were good enough for them to proceed with my second round of chemotherapy that day. When I was finished receiving blood, I would be moved to the room where I would live while I received my treatment.

When I had received all of the blood products they had for me, I was placed on the fifth floor to receive treatment. Although I had requested four tower where I had been for my last stay, all of the rooms on that floor were full. So, for the time being, I would be on the fifth floor. I was wheeled onto the fifth floor in a wheel chair with Blake behind me, pushing me along. The fifth floor had a completely different lay out than the fourth floor. The fifth floor was more bare than my beloved four tower, traces that children were even there were few. Only the stray wagon sitting next to the nurse's station with paintings of rainbows on it acknowledged the presence of children. The fourth floor had pictures painted by children hanging everywhere and the nurse's station was always decorated. There was even a playroom at the end of the fourth floor hallway. The fifth floor was in some ways more serious and cold than the fourth floor, I didn't like it. My parents had walked ahead of Blake and I. Blake and I took our time walking around the hallways and getting acquainted with our new floor. By the time Blake wheeled me into our room, my mom had already made my bed with my sheets and blankets from home. She had even covered the mattress with a special down mattress cover to make it more comfortable. I climbed into my bed while my family busied themselves setting the room up around me. Once my parents were acquainted with the nursing staff and had situated and sterilized my room to their satisfaction, they left Blake and I to be alone until the morning. I definitely didn't like the room that I was in as much as I liked my room on the fourth floor. I didn't like the bare walls. In my old room, I felt at home, in this room, I felt like I was in a hospital receiving treatment for cancer. Blake and I tried to busy ourselves by playing a game together on our computers, but Blake seemed impatient. He picked up the phone in our room and called down to the nurse's station on the fourth floor. He asked to speak to Angela or Catherine; which ever was on duty at that time, the nurse that picked up the phone put him on hold. The next voice we heard was Catherine. As soon as Blake heard her speak he said, "Hey, it's Blake and Charlie, is there a room down there yet?" Catherine told us that it was highly likely that one would come open in the next thirty minutes and that she would call us back as soon as she found us a room on the fourth floor. My parents hadn't been gone long when Blake and I got a phone call from sweet Nurse Catherine and found out that a room on the fourth floor had opened up and we could have it. Blake asked if we could come down right away and she told him that the staff at the hospital had already cleaned it and the old bed was moved out so they would send someone up to roll my bed down when they got a chance. Blake didn't want to wait so he told her that he could handle it and just asked her to make sure the nurses on the fifth floor knew that we were transferring. He hung up the phone and put his computer away. Blake grabbed our bags and ran them down to our new room on the fourth floor. He left me in bed, promising to return quickly. When he got back to the room he maneuvered my bed around so that he could push it out and into our new room. I assumed that normally someone from the hospital would be required to move a patient in their bed, but I figured Catherine had already notified someone at the hospital of what we were doing and I hadn't started treatment or anything yet, so none of my IVs were attached. Either way, he successfully wheeled me, bed, and all down to our new room on the fourth floor. Usually, when a patient is moved in bed, they will travel on the staff elevators. However, we weren't staff and had no way of getting on the staff elevators since they required a special code. Since it was very late at night, the public elevators were unoccupied, which was lucky for us because I don't think we would have been able to get my bed on a public elevator in that hospital at any other time of the day. During the day, the elevators were always full with people and it seemed like no matter how many times the elevators stopped on the different floors, there were always people waiting to get on and every elevator was always full of staff and visitors.

As Blake wheeled me out of the elevator and down the dimly lit hallway, I searched for signs of life on my home floor. I knew that when the lights were darkened in the hallways, most of the patients were asleep for the night. As we got further down the hallway, bright light from the nurse's station illuminated the area just ahead of us on the right. As Blake wheeled me by, my nurses, including Catherine smiled and laughed at my brother and I. I liked to think that they were always more entertained when we were there. I stared at the blue square mounted on the wall next to the door I was being pushed into. In white numbers, I read out the room number, four fifty-six. I didn't get room four forty-four, which was sad for me, but I was aware before I even came back that room four forty-four would probably not be available for me. My new room, room four fifty-six, was just a little smaller than four forty-four and the bathroom was on the opposite side of the room. Also, four fifty-six was further down the hallway; pass the nurse's station. However, I was content just being on the fourth floor with my nurses.

As I had expected, my second stay in the hospital was nothing like my first stay. The chemotherapy I was receiving was a lot more difficult for my body to handle than it was during my first induction round. My body was still responding well to the medicine, but unfortunately I felt much sicker during second induction. I couldn't eat because I was constantly nauseous and when I did eat, everything had that weird chemotherapy taste to it. My nurses tried to suggest foods that might taste better than what I had been eating, but there wasn't anything else they could do, the taste was just a side effect of the chemotherapy.

I didn't leave my room at all during my second stay. I never felt well enough. I had fewer visitors than I did the first time as well; my immediate family was my main company. One of the best visitors I had during my second stay was Jonah, the boy I met in clinic just a few days before I was admitted for my second stay that had leukemia too. The day I saw Jonah on the fourth floor, my mom and brother were sitting with me as I struggled to eat another meal they had presented me with. My mom left the room to my door open as she went to get a drink for me from the parent's lounge. While she was gone, I could hear laughter and commotion in the hallway right outside my door. Once those sounds had died down, I heard squeaky wheels coming in my direction. Before I knew it, Jonah was sitting in front of my door on a red tricycle. He wasn't wearing a shirt or shoes and had on pajama pants, I noticed that he had not yet lost his hair, he smiled proudly at me. "Hey Jonah!" I greeted him. He spoke back to me as clearly as he could for his three years of age. As I was trying to understand what he was telling me, his mother walked up behind him. I smiled at her.

"He's going downstairs today because the volunteer clowns will be here to play and he wants to know if you're going to come too." She said, smiling back at me.

"Oh, no, sorry Jonah, I'm having my chemotherapy today."

"Yeah, I know how that is." He said in a more serious, grown up way than I had heard him speak before. He squeaked away on his tricycle and his mom chased behind him. My brother and I couldn't help but laugh as we watched him wheel away. He had so much energy and was so happy even though he was receiving some very difficult treatment, the way he hung his head down and spoke those words with true wisdom and knowledge really struck me. Although, he knew the pain that I was feeling and he knew he would feel it again, he still kept that same happy view of the world that every child has. I used that little interaction for inspiration as I continued on my journey. The world should take a lesson from little children like Jonah. Jonah knows that sometimes there is pain and sadness in life, but he never dwells on it because he is too busy seeking out the happiness. When I felt really sick and I started to think that I would never feel better, I would think about Jonah and laugh and remember how fleeting pain is and then I would find my happiness.

Boredom combined with constant confinement during our first and second stays in the hospital prompted my brother and I to come up with new and more interesting ways of entertaining ourselves. During one of my last nights of my second stay in the hospital, I was feeling well and energetic, but the medical staff had forbidden me from most activities because all of my counts were low. I had low platelets, white blood cells, and red blood cells. I lay in bed; bored with the video game I had been playing. I stared at the blinking red light on the camera that my Uncle Perry had given me much earlier in my diagnosis. It was in its usual place on a tripod angled at my bed, watching my every move. That camera had become both mine and my brother's constant companion, it was a rare occasion when that camera was not on and recording. Watching the red light, I thought of all of our hilarious antics it had caught on tape. My brother and I were proudly known as the entertainment on our floor. It wouldn't be rare to see a huddle of doctors and nurses standing in the doorway of my room laughing. Often, my medical team would visit with me much longer than they had planned. Once they had finished telling me the news of the day, they would stay and listen to me talk. I had become like a stand-up comedian, cancer patient, my stage was the hospital. I knew I would be leaving the hospital soon, and I wanted to get one good prank in before I left. I looked over at my brother who was busy typing away on his large, glowing laptop.

"What time is it?" I asked him.

"About seven, why?" He replied with out even looking up from the screen.

"Since it's night shift, Catherine's probably here. Get up, I want to trick her when she comes in!"

Now that I knew what time it was, I knew that my night nurse, Catherine would be coming in to do her first check with me within the next thirty minutes. If we were going to pull the prank off, we had to hurry. Blake was standing next to my bed; as soon as I told him to get up he had jumped to his feet. I hung my feet over the side of my bed and explained the plan for our last prank for that stay. Blake would get in my bed and cover himself with my blanket so just the back of his bald head would be revealed, Blake had kept his head bald since he first shaved his hair off with me, and I would lay on the cot where Blake usually slept and cover myself with his blankets. When Catherine came in to do her check she would think we were sleeping and try to do the normal tests and checks I received on Blake because she would think that he was me and the camera would catch her reaction on tape. Catherine was loud and out-going and her reactions always suited her personality, she was one of the best nurses to joke around with. Blake, of course, was excited about my plan, but he had to make sure that I would be safe and no germs would be transferred from him to me. The first thing he did was grab the hand-sanitizer that he kept on the nightstand in the hospital room and hurriedly cleaned his hands. He pulled his blankets and pillows off his tiny makeshift bed and laid them on a chair next to the door. He walked to the closet and pulled out a sterile sheet and then gently draped it over the cot he had been laying on. He turned to me and told me to lie on the cot, I did, and he laid my blanket on top of me. He then handed me all three of my pillows. He went back to the closet and grabbed another sterile sheet that he used to drape over my bed. Once he felt comfortable that he wouldn't infect my bed, he went to the light switches and turned all of the lights off. He then walked to the sink and turned the dim light over top of it on. As he clicked the light on, we thought we heard the door opening, Blake turned and leaped into my bed and hurriedly covered himself perfectly with blankets. However, we laid and giggled for what seemed like a lifetime while we waited on Catherine to arrive.

Finally, we heard a knock on the door. We didn't answer because we were trying to keep up the guise that we were sleeping; we tried to quiet our laughter. I heard the door squeak open and peeked out into the darkness from under my blanket and saw the light streaming in from the hallway. I watched Catherine walk over to the bed and lay her hand on Blake. I watched her face become a little confused as she began to pull the blanket back, I saw Blake's face, smiling and I couldn't help the loud laugh that came out. Catherine jumped back from Blake with a shocked look on her face and then we all broke into uncontrollable laughter.

The next day, I was released from the hospital. I only ended up staying at the hospital that time for about a week. During the stay, I had fewer visitors, and because everyone knew I wouldn't be staying for long, my hospital room remained bare. Instead of being turned into a surrogate home for me as room four forty-four was, it was left as a bare hospital room. When my nurse practitioner came in to tell me that I would be able to finish chemotherapy at home this time, I was elated. The entire week of second induction was a nauseating blur. At times, when I felt good enough, I would play games on my computer. For the most part, however, my head was in a bucket as I watched my family come in and out day after day. The chemotherapy I would be receiving at home would not be as hard on me as the medicines I was receiving in the hospital so for that simple fact alone, I was thankful.

I smiled at my nurse, Angela, as my big brother pushed me down the hallway of the fourth floor as he had done so many times before. I was going home, again. Of course, being a cancer patient, I always kept in my mind that I could be coming back at any moment. However, for the time being, I was thankful and happy to be going home. I put the elastic bands of my mask around my ears as my brother wheeled me in to a crowded elevator. People smiled at us, but their smiles seemed sad. Blake turned me around so that I could face the front of the elevator like everyone else. He pressed the number two and it lit up.

When the elevator doors opened up, Blake wheeled me out to my mom's car where my parents were waiting for me. When the sliding glass door opened up and I felt the rush of cold wind hit me from the outside, I felt a lively jolt. I hadn't been outside, nonetheless, felt the wind in days, I felt really alive that day. Although it was painfully cold, I soaked up every second of being out in the world; I knew that it wouldn't last forever. I climbed in the front seat of my mom's black SUV and Blake shut the door behind me. As we drove away, I stared out of my window at the hospital until I couldn't see it anymore.

When we finally made it home, I felt tired. Blake and I went straight to my room and lay down for the night. We knew that more than likely we wouldn't stay asleep. Pretty soon, I would be woken up to receive my first dose of in-home chemotherapy.

I was still asleep when my parents came in and turned my bedside lamp on. It was the late evening hours and my exhausted parents who always had a look of fear in their eyes were about to give me chemo on their own for the first time. I woke up because I could hear plastic tearing and packages being opened on the right side of my bed. I was still halfway asleep as I rolled myself over and pushed my eyes open. My mom and dad had a small table they had set up by my bed, it was covered with sterile medical utensils, my dad was wearing rubber gloves. My mom looked over and saw that I was awake, "Just keep on sleeping, honey. Daddy and me are going to clean your central line and give you a dose of your medicine. You need to rest."

"I love you Mommy." I said as I kept watching them.

"I love you too Charlie." She said as she rubbed my arm.

Eventually, Dad was ready to administer my medicine. My mom pulled my blankets down and I rolled onto my back. I pulled my shirt off so that my parents could get to my central line just like I had for my nurses when they administered my medicine in the hospital. I was an old pro at chemotherapy, my parents were rookies. Dad started to lean over me to begin sterilizing my line and then he pulled back. He had forgotten to put on a mask, he was aware that if he breathed on my central line it could become infected, and if he breathed on the equipment he was using, it could become contaminated and we would be unable to use it. He slid the bands of the mask over his ears and leaned back over my chest to get back to work. I lay on my back and looked up at the ceiling while my dad concentrated on cleaning my line. Before I got the line, I thought it would hurt to have it cleaned. I had actually become accustomed to the two tubes sticking out of my chest, known as my central line. As Dad cleaned it, I could feel pressure and slight tugs every now and then, but it was never painful. The chemotherapy was the painful part. Sometimes I didn't know what was worse, the disease or the treatment for the disease. It was hard to see the pain in my strong father's eyes. He was a physician and had diagnosed people with cancer and terminal illnesses before, but I can't imagine what it was like for him to have to diagnose his own son. I knew that he had knowledge that was an advantage over other parents that were caring for children with serious illnesses because of his medical education, but at the same time I believe that his knowledge was also a disadvantage because he knew the cold hard truth of what this disease was all about, he understood and had seen what this disease could do to a person and now he was having to watch me struggle with it. I watched him carefully sterilize the end of my central line and he slowly began to inject my chemotherapy. When he was finished, he sterilized again and then carefully placed a bandage over my central line. The medications that were used to ease the side effects of the chemo I had just taken were lying on my bedside table. I rolled over and tried to fall asleep, I hoped I wouldn't need that medicine that was sitting on my bedside table.

When I woke up the next morning, I felt better than I had since I started my second round of chemo. I lay there in bed looking at the ceiling and thinking about all of the changes that had occurred in my life since I was diagnosed with cancer. I knew that something greater was at work in this world. This morning, I felt peace. I felt that I could see my life more clearly. I looked at my life, while my brother lay in the floor beside me sleeping, objectively, like a bystander.

I used to wake up every morning eager and excited to start the day, mostly because every night before I fell asleep, I lay in bed, sometimes for hours, and imagined what my future would be like. I tried to see myself in the future, what goals would I accomplish? What would I have to do the next day to get closer to those dreams? Most of the time, my dreams always boiled down to basketball.

I always wanted to be the best; I was willing to do what it took to be on top. I wanted to shine on the court and get recruited to play at a big division college, maybe the University of Kentucky, since they're my family's team. I thought about going pro, but decided that I really wanted to coach. On and on I would dream and my dreams got bigger and bigger, but being diagnosed with cancer made all of that different.

"You know sometimes I wake up and I don't know I have cancer because, somehow, in my sleep, I forget that I have cancer, then when I remember, 'oh, yeah, I have cancer,' I get sad." I said in a truthful, but joking way to my big brother as he lay on the cot in my bedroom floor. I was lying in my bed and we had just woken up.

He laughed a little and said, "I do that too, but I remember that you have cancer, it sucks."

It was true. I always wanted to keep a positive attitude, but sometimes I had to work hard to do that. Cancer's not an easy thing for anyone to deal with. Before cancer, I dreamt of a future. Now that I have cancer, I can't do that. I know that there may not be a tomorrow. I also know that more than likely I will wake up in my well-sterilized house and be a prisoner inside of it, that is, if I don't get sick and wake up in the hospital.

I still dream about what the future may be like, but I don't dream of the same things anymore. Now, I try to imagine graduating from high school. I see myself sitting on the football field in my cap and gown, the warm, May air sticking to my skin. I can smell the freshly cut grass and hear my principle speaking about my graduating class and wishing us well in the future. But most importantly, I can look up in the stadium and see my family looking back down at me. They were all there, my mom, my dad, Blake, Tab, and Chandler.

I dream of myself standing in a hospital, looking through the thick glass window of a nursery. I can see her, lying in her crib, she smiles at me. Her pink blanket wrapped tightly around her tiny little body. The sign on the bottom of her bed has my name on it. She's mine, who doesn't want to be a parent some day? How wonderful it would be to have a little person that is just like you and loves you more than life. I make eye contact with the small baby and we smile as if we've known each other all along. I felt so happy to be there in that moment, I wondered if I would make it there.

I dream of seeing a beautiful girl walk down the aisle of a church adorned in flowers, she's dressed all in white. I imagine what it might be like to get married. I can feel myself holding a soft, small hand. A hand that I knew I would be holding forever, she was my wife and it was my wedding day. I was standing at the front of the church looking out into the congregation. All familiar faces, my mom and dad were crying tears of joy. I see friends and old teammates. Then I look beside me at my two brothers Blake and Chandler and my best friend Eddie, I looked at the bridesmaids, but the only one I recognized was my sister, she was smiling as tears ran down her face, I was doing the same thing.

There were so many things I wanted to experience still in life. I wanted to be there for my nieces and nephews that I knew would soon come along, I wanted to be Uncle Charlie. I wanted to be there when my brothers and my sister got married. I wanted to be called dad. I wanted to get married. I wanted to graduate from high school and college and I wanted to be there when Chandler did those things too. I wanted to grow up with the rest of my family, but I knew that I might not ever get that chance.

So, as I wake up every morning and the eagerness I feel for the day is disrupted by thoughts of what might not be, I know I have to focus on the here and now. That's all any of us can do. I have cancer, I'm not dead yet. I can still fight it and at least I get that chance. At least I actually get to live in the moment knowing that tomorrow isn't promised, that's something that most people never get to do. Nobody is promised tomorrow and we all leave this world eventually. At least I get the opportunity to truly live with that knowledge everyday and in turn I know to take full advantage of every second I have alive on this earth.

After being released from the hospital, I spent most of my days at home. I still had the eagerness to get out and be with friends. Eddie helped those feelings subside by spending most every day with my brother and I, playing on our computers and making light conversation with each other. I loved having Eddie there because I knew as long as I took a mask and stayed in his truck I could go out to where my friends were or even go get my own food from whatever restaurant I pleased. The normal, natural way of living I was used to could continue in this way. However, I knew that basketball season had started and I was hoping that there could be a way for me to go watch my teams play. My medical staff at Children's Hospital had adamantly restricted me to stay away from places with crowds like gymnasiums at basketball games. However, that didn't stop my desire to go.

Eventually my desire grew so strong that I had to ask my family if they thought there would be anyway I could attend a couple of basketball games. The ones that were most important to me were for Dora High School, the team my favorite coach, Coach Burns was coaching. Coach Burns had been my coach during my favorite years so far in my basketball career, seventh and eighth grade. Our team had been outstanding those years, and I was MVP. I looked up to Coach Burns and believed in him, we had a strong connection as player and coach. I knew that in just a few days, they would be playing at my old high school, which was less than ten minutes from my house. I was eager to see it. I explained my desire to see these games to my dad. To my surprise, he was excited to give me the chance to go to all of the games. He called my brother and sister into my room where we were talking. We sat together, devising a plan for how I could attend with out causing any damage to my already compromised condition.

It was decided that for the first game, my brother, cousin, and sister would take me to the game and my dad and Uncle Perry would meet us there when they could leave work. Blake and Tab would stand in the crowd to buy tickets and explain at the ticket booth, our situation. They would then walk around to the side door of the gymnasium where my cousin and I would be waiting. We would walk up the farthest side of the bleachers to the very top where our backs were against the wall so that no one could stand over me. My siblings and my cousin would form a wide circle around me to keep anyone else from getting near to me. Once this plan was set, I was allowed to go to the game. I wondered if that was what it took to go out if you were a celebrity. It was amusing to me that I had my own security team, even if it was because I had cancer.

My sister came to me after we had discussed the plan to take me to the game and asked if there was any way I would change my mind and stay home. She was scared that it was too dangerous and I would get sick.

"Tab," I responded, "Going to this game means more to me than going to the NBA playoffs."

She looked at me with a defeated and worried expression and said, "Well, alright, I guess we're going."

I heard the loud buzz of the scoreboard as I stood in the December cold with my cousin, Alex, who was trying his best to coerce me to put my mask on. I refused, assuring him that I would be fine. I hated wearing those masks, I was trying to keep people from noticing me there, and wearing a surgical mask would make me stick out like a soar thumb. I looked up and saw the police officer working the game approaching the glass door my cousin and I were standing at. As he got closer, I realized that I knew him. He opened the door; suspicious that we were trying to sneak into the game.

"Can I help you boys?" He asked in an authoritative tone.

Alex began to try and explain our situation, but I quickly took over. I pulled the hood I had on down to uncover my head to show him who I was. "It's me, Charlie. My brother and sister are buying my ticket now, but I'm sick and I can't be around people so I have to come in this way."

"Oh, yeah. Well, come on. Get out of the cold." He said as he held the door open for us just in time to see my brother and sister come around the corner.

Once we were seated we knew our plan had succeeded. Now, I could enjoy the game. It wasn't long before my dad and my Uncle Perry showed up, making the large entourage surrounding me a little larger. A few of my friends spotted me from across the gym and walked over to say hello, each one was stopped by one of my family members before they could get close to me. They would all stop and stand from their distance and we would shout our greetings at one another. Coach Burns' team didn't win so I was a little disappointed, but just getting to go to the game and having the sensation of a real basketball game happening around me lifted my spirits tremendously. I wished I could be playing out there with those other boys, but this was the next best thing.

Once the game was over, my family and I stayed seated in our positions and waited for the crowd to exit. I watched the seas of people pouring out of doors on either side of the gym; it was odd that I couldn't just exit along with them. Eventually, the gym was cleared and my family escorted me out the side door of the gym that I had walked in through.

Chris, Tab, me and Chan at Ice in Nashville Christmas 2007.

The Most Wonderful Time of the Year

Eventually preparations for Christmas were in full swing. I had asked my family to wait until I got home to decorate the big family Christmas tree that we always sat in the corner of our family room. I was disappointed to see that it was up and decorated when I got home from the hospital, but after careful inspection, I realized that it wasn't decorated with our traditional ornaments. My cousin had used makeshift decorations to put on it temporarily until I came home to help decorate the tree with the rest of my family, as was our tradition. The wooden rails along our stairs were decorated with garland and white lights, and the white spindles underneath them were wrapped with red ribbon so that they looked like candy canes. The top of the fireplace was covered with fake snow and a tiny village, our stocking holders sat out, bare and waiting to be accented with a stuffed stocking on Christmas morning.

A life-sized, furry statue of The Grinch sat in our foyer with a wreath over his head, ready to greet all visitors who dare enter the crazy Lovely household. Every room in the house had a Christmas tree; mine was the biggest, besides the family tree. We decorated my tree with blue ornaments and blue lights and we topped it off with a blue bow, underneath my mom had placed a blue and white tree skirt. We also had a white and blue, Kentucky tree given to me by my Uncle David's wife, my Aunt Sherry that sat up on the fireplace in the center of the little snow town. Even the outside of our house was littered with Christmas decorations.

We had a wreath on every window, lights all over the house; blow up snowman decorations, and not to mention "HO HO HO" written on our door with red wooden letters. Needless to say, our house was literally a winter wonderland.

My sister and mother made many Christmas shopping trips that year on their breaks from sanitizing the house. This year I was excited about Christmas, but it wasn't the same as it had been before. I used to have such carefree, happy feelings about the Holidays. Now, however, I felt it hard to experience those same kinds of feelings. Although Christmas time was still happy for me and I enjoyed spending the holidays with my family in our little winter wonderland we had created, I, as I am sure my family did as well, had a continuous feeling of fear and uncertainty hanging over me.

These feelings, for me, stemmed from the worry of getting sick. I knew that it was almost impossible to keep from contracting some kind of virus or sickness, I had already been told that I would more than likely be coming back to the hospital with a fever any day. It was hard to stay well with a compromised immune system and I wanted to at least make it through Christmas before having to go back to the hospital, not so much for me, but for my family, especially my litter brother, Chan.

I had been home for a little over two weeks when Christmas Eve fell, I had been back and forth to Birmingham for short clinic visits through out that time, but I actually felt pretty free from my hospital life. I woke up that day excited that I had already made it so far with out getting sick and in less than twenty-four hours I would be opening up presents under the Christmas tree in our beloved family room with Chandler and the rest of my family. Just the thought of a moment like that made me feel a sense of accomplishment. However, that fear and uncertainty still hung over me, I knew that I could get sick and have to go back to the hospital before the morning came. I had woken up feeling a little less well than I had been feeling. I was pretty sluggish and my throat was a little soar, but I shrugged it off. I assumed I was probably tired since I hadn't been sleeping much and I didn't want to alarm anyone.

Christmas Eve morning was always special in my family. Mom cooked a big breakfast with bacon, eggs, biscuits, and all the other glories of a good old-fashioned southern breakfast. I woke up to the sweet smell of bacon cooking. My whole family gathered in the kitchen in our pajamas. We all ate and then sat around the living room together watching our favorite Christmas movies to get into the spirit. It was really special to me that I got to spend that time with them; I knew how lucky I was to be there in that moment. I had made it to Christmas Eve. The only thing that would have made it better would have been if Dad had been there, but he was working and I knew he wasn't happy about missing it either.

That morning was so crisp and fresh, it wasn't snowing outside, but the temperature outside was fairly cold for Alabama weather. The sun was shining down through the trees in our backyard. Its rays danced all over their limbs as they blew in the wind. I was glad to be inside and warm with my family. Mom made us hot chocolate and then my sister cooked a lunch of vegetable soup and grilled cheese. That lunch was my request, I had started eating more soup since I was diagnosed. My family and I had been trying to make sure I had plenty of vegetables and good healthy food to eat everyday. I love vegetable soup, so it was an easy way to eat healthy and still enjoy my food.

Once our stomachs were full with hot chocolate and all of the other food the women in my family had cooked that day, the drowsiness began to set in. All of us, except for my sister, went off to our respective rooms to nap. Blake, of course, slept on the little mattress beside my bed.

When I woke up about two hours later, I knew that I was sick. My whole body ached and I was severely nauseated. I was so tired that I could barely speak to ask my brother for some water. After a couple of sad and quiet attempts to wake him up over the noise of our box fan, my drowsiness overcame me and I fell back asleep.

When I woke up again, my mom was standing over me with a thermometer. She had been trying to wake me up.

"Charlie, you feel really hot and your face is flushed. I need to take your temperature now." I opened up my mouth. I was too tired and sick to do anything else. I didn't even feel like talking. We waited anxiously to hear the beep of the thermometer. When it finally beeped, the look on my mom's face told me it wasn't good.

"You're temperature is 104.7. Let's get to the hospital." She said in the way a soldier might say "Let's get to the battlefield" to his fellow soldiers before they march into the war zone.

Blake immediately jumped into action. He grabbed the bag that we already had packed for me in case that I would have to be rushed to the hospital, which we were basically told was inevitable. My mom ran into the kitchen to call my dad and grab whatever else we might need. It took most of my strength to sit myself up in the bed. Once I was sitting up I began feeling dizzy, I knew it would be too difficult for me to walk around and change my clothes and prepare myself to leave on my own. I told my brother what I wanted to wear and he brought it to me. I first slipped off the shirt I was wearing stained with some of the soup my sister had made me earlier in the day. I put on my Burn's Ballers shirt, which was given to me by Coach Burns at the last basketball game I had attended. Coach Burns reserved my family a sectioned off area so that we could freely come to his games with out worry of me being put into a crowd of people. I loved that shirt, and I was pleased that everyone in my family had gotten one too.

Once I had my shirt on, I leaned back in the bed to slip my pants off and put on the clean black sweat pants my brother had brought me. I pulled the socks I was wearing off at the same time I slid my pants off. I leaned over and picked up my clean pants and once more mustered up the strength to lean back and pull my pants up. Once I had finished these grueling tasks I felt like I could pass out at any moment. I was nauseous, the room was spinning, and I was light headed. I told my brother, who was sitting in the floor of my room stuffing whatever extra things he thought I might need into my duffel bag, that I was concerned that I could pass out. He, of course being the second year medical student and wanting to try on his own to figure out what was wrong with me started tossing the usual questions at me when I mentioned I was sick, "Do you feel nauseous?"

"Yes," I answered.

He got up to grab a bucket to put near me in case I needed to throw up.

"Do you feel dizzy or light headed at all?" he asked.

"Yes."

"Okay, just stay sitting like you are and relax, try to focus on breathing." He grabbed my socks and slid them on my feet. He grabbed my shoes from behind him and slowly slipped them on my feet one by one. I helped him as much as I could.

"Can you get this on yourself, or do you need help?" He asked, holding up my favorite red, fleece jacket.

"I'll put it on." I said as he tossed it to me. My sister walked in wiping her hands down. She didn't say anything to us and we didn't say anything to her. There was nothing to say. I got my jacket on, and Blake helped me stand up.

"Hey Tab, you're going to have to help me too. I'm real weak." I said to my sister. She rushed to my side and put her arms around me. The three of us, my two older siblings and I began a slow and steady walk out of our home. Blake was on my right with my bag slung over his right shoulder; Tab was on my left holding me with both arms. Blake had to let go to run back in and grab some other things that he didn't want me to leave behind, leaving Tab to help me down the stairs, through our garage and out to our mom's car by her self. I was a little scared at first that surely she wouldn't be able to hold me up if I were to collapse. Even though I was six years younger, I was far bigger than her in size. However, it only took a few seconds for me to realize how strong her arms felt as she held on to me and led me down the stairs, with me reminding her the whole way to remember I could fall at any time. I trusted her arms like I trusted my mothers, I knew that no matter what she had to do, I would be safe with her, she wouldn't let me fall. I heard Chandler's footsteps in the house behind me. I guess he realized what was happening when he saw Tab half-carrying me out of our home. He started crying as he ran upstairs to his room.

"I'm sorry, Chan." I shouted behind me, before I stepped out of my house.

My big sister pulled my hood up over my head as we began making our way out of the garage; I bent my head down to focus on my steps and avoid the pelting rain. I watched my sister's small feet walk beside mine, she was only wearing socks and they were now soaking wet. I was soon seated safely inside of my mom's car with my bucket in between my knees. My brother jumped in beside me and my sister ran back in our house to take care of Chandler. My mom ran out to the car, jumped in the driver's seat, and sped out of our driveway.

Before I knew it, we were pulling into the parking lot of a grocery store in our town; I saw my dad's truck sitting in one of the parking spaces. My mom jumped over into the passenger seat and my dad jumped into the driver's seat and off we sped again. I laid my head back and closed my eyes trying to keep myself focused on not getting sick in the car. My stomach was killing me and although I had begun to sweat, I was freezing. At one point I looked at the speedometer and it read ninety-eight miles per hour. I couldn't believe how fast we were going.

No one spoke, except for my brother who would question me about how I was feeling every few minutes. I was miserable and holding on with all I had until we made it to the hospital. Eventually I felt the turning motions of the car and I knew we were in the parking garage of the hospital. My brother had his door open and was getting out of the car before we had even stopped. He ran around to my side and helped me get out, as soon as I stepped out of the car, I vomited. I knew it was coming, but thankfully I had been able to control it long enough for us to make it to the hospital. Blake held my little bucket in front of me as I continued to throw up. Eventually, it subsided, and I started to try to catch my breath.

"Are you done or do you need to throw up some more?" Blake questioned me. I was leaning over with my hands on my thighs.

"I'm done." I murmured. I looked up to see my dad rolling a wheel chair over to me. I sat down and rested my feet on the pedals. I put my mask on at my mom's request. Blake was pushing me, and I was holding my vomit bucket in my lap. They wheeled me into the hospital, Blake pushing, and my mom and dad on either side.

Once we made it into the hospital, the doctors on staff in the emergency room read my chart and immediately sent me to PICU. Because of my compromised immune system I couldn't be anywhere else. They didn't know what I was sick with, but the doctors know when they see a bald kid, their immune system probably isn't up to the challenge of fighting off any sickness on its own.

My mom fixed a hospital bed for me, complete with my mattress pad, my sheets from home and my favorite blanket. Soon workers at the hospital were in the emergency room, ready to wheel me down to PICU. I lay in my bed, my piece of home with a lady on either side of me. I looked up at the ceiling tiles as I was wheeled to an already familiar place to me. I began experiencing serious déjà vu as I was being wheeled through the hallways. I had been wheeled through those hallways before, but somehow I felt like I could remember this exact situation, this exact moment happening before. My mom was walking beside me; she knew that I had already experienced déjà vu in the hospital before. I looked over at her and murmured through my sickness, "Mom, I'm having déjà vu again. I know this has happened before."

She rubbed my head, "It's okay Charlie, just think of déjà vu as a way of the Lord telling you that you're on the right path and you're where you should be." I smiled at her; a mother's words will always relieve even the most scared and weary soul.

In the PICU at the hospital I was at, there were only two glassed in rooms for children with compromised immune systems. Instead of getting thirteen, this time I was wheeled into the next glass door down, room ten. The workers positioned my bed to where it faced out of the glassed in room, where I could see sullen-eyed visitors walking in and out to see the other occupants of this strange place. My family had walked in with me to help me get situated in my new room. It was late at night by this point, and I was feeling quite drowsy. The nurses explained to my family that it wasn't visiting hours and they would have to wait until midnight to come back in and see me.

Since my last stay in the PICU, my mother had become very familiar with PICU visiting hours. She knew that with how sick I was, I would need her with me all night. My brother and father walked out to the waiting room, but my mother stayed back and eventually coerced the nurse into letting her stay through the night. Because of my condition, everyone was required to be fully dressed in gowns, gloves, and masks before entering my room. The nurse I had been assigned to I had never met before, I watched her as she pulled two large plastic containers full of the sanitary dresses next to my door. I then watched her lay two boxes of gloves and two boxes of mask on top of these plastic containers. I watched Mom get suited up, and the nurse led her into my room. I was glad my mom had fought to stay with me. I knew she would.

The nurse showed my mom where everything she may need in the room was. I watched my mom try to stuff the knowledge of the contents of every drawer in the room into her mind. Packs of petroleum jelly were in the far left drawer on top, gauze was in the middle drawers, and so on. When the nurse was finished giving my mom the tutorial of the room, she asked if there was anything else she could do for her, my mom nodded her head, and the nurse walked out of my room. She slid the glass door shut behind her and I noticed two big stickers of Disney princes in the center of the door. My mom pulled the curtains closed and I never saw them vividly again. I soon tried to sleep in between doses of antibiotics and anti-nausea medication. Nothing seemed to work. I was dizzy, but had to get up and down all night to use the restroom. Each time my mom had to help me get in and out of my bed. I woke up out of my sleep quite often to vomit in the bucket my mom was holding beside me. The one constant I knew would be there when I woke up was my mom. Every time I opened my eyes I saw her right beside me wide-eyed and ready to try and save me from whatever was making me sick. Most of the time, unless she was reading to me from the Bible, I never even had to open my eyes to know she was there beside me. No matter how old you get, the loving touch of your mother always seems to make everything feel better. Maybe somehow, subconsciously, my mother knew this, because she rarely let her right hand move from me. I would close my eyes again after recognizing her beside me and fall back asleep, even for just a moment, as my mother rubbed my hand with hers.

I had been in severe pain through out the night. Nothing the medical staff did seemed to help my condition. The doctors were unsure of what was causing me to be so sick. They had started me on a steady course of antibiotics under the assumption that I more than likely had some sort of virus. Of course, they still voiced their fears that I may have an infection. A virus is the most normal thing for chemo patients to have, they can become much sicker than the regular person do to their compromised immune system. I knew from listening to my brother and dad that a bacterial infection would be bad news and was a great fear for them because it is more likely to result in fatality or death. My fever had gone down, but my temperature was still high. I lay with the covers pulled completely off my body and my mom and the nurses had put cool wet cloths on my body, a box fan that was sitting on the table to my left blew a constant breeze directly at me, it was one of my only reliefs.

I had heard the nurse that was on duty during my first shift mention to my mom that I could possibly have contracted c-diff or clostridium difficile, which is a bacterium that causes diarrhea and serious intestinal conditions, rarely does c-diff result in death. In fact, I had visited my friend, Jonah, who was three the last time I came to clinic and he was in with c-diff, but he didn't seem to be as sick as I had gotten. Even though I was in severe pain, it eased me to know that it wasn't fatal, and I'm sure it eased my mom too.

Eventually, I had gone for over twenty-four hours with out eating. Not to mention, the only sleep I had were short naps in between vomiting spells. I had little to throw up anymore, but my stomach still convulsed with nausea. I was on several different antibiotics and was taking different medications for nausea. My mom tried to feed me crackers and Sprite, but I couldn't keep anything down and eating was anything but attractive to me. I began dreaming, and my family told me that I would talk during my fits of sleep. I must have been hallucinating or somewhat conscious, but I didn't remember saying or doing anything they told me about. I remembered dreaming about Chandler a lot. I was so worried about how he was; we had never gone so long with out seeing each other as we had since I had been diagnosed.

I worried that I had ruined Christmas for him, and he didn't understand why I couldn't stay home. I would dream that he was standing beside me asking me to play with him, and even though I was sleeping I still felt sick, so in my dream I would tell him to get his dog, Toby, and play with him. I would dream that he was begging me to come home with him, and I never could figure out how he had gotten into my room because we were always alone and I knew that Chandler was too young to be allowed back into the PICU. He would just stare at me and say, "Just come home, Char. Just come home." And that was it.

When I wasn't sick or having hallucinations and dreams, I would stare at the round, black clock hanging on the right wall of my small glass hospital room. I watched the small second hand tick, tick, tick its way around the clock over and over again. As hours would pass, I would become more and more desperate to get out of that PICU. I would ask my mom every once in a while, when she thought I would be going back to the fourth floor. She would just turn her eyes to the ground and nod her head and say, "I don't know, Charlie. I don't know."

My mom had stayed in my glass room in the PICU with me for over thirty-six hours straight when she was finally asked to leave. She begged and pleaded to stay with me, and I wanted her to stay with me so badly, but hospital staff had set strict hours for PICU and even my mom had to stick to those hours. She cried as they made her leave. It was hard for me to see her leave too, but I didn't cry. I needed her; the comfort of her being there was better than any medicine the doctor could give me. Now, I was alone, I would lie in bed with my bucket beside me and stare through the glass windows around me. I always focused on the double doors that lead into the PICU, eagerly waiting to see one of my family members walk through the door. I always felt relief when I would see them come in. I would watch them wash their hands and suit up to stay with me for the short two hours we would have together. I didn't want to take my eyes off of them; it felt too good to see them there.

When I was in the room alone. I would lie in bed for as long as I could, hoping that I would last until the next set of visiting hours before having to go the restroom on my own. I never made it, and it was always difficult to get out of bed and use the makeshift toilet that they had set up beside my bed since I was too weak to walk to the bathroom. I had IVs in both arms and my central line was always tangled in something. I was delirious, but I knew how careful I had to be. I was aware that not only was my immune system broke down because of chemotherapy, but I had almost no platelets, so it wouldn't take much for me to bleed to death if I fell because I couldn't hold myself or if I pulled any of my cords out. I would use the bathroom as quickly as possible so that I could lie back down in bed. When I was upright, I felt extremely dizzy. I was always relieved when I fell back into my hospital bed, but I knew that I wouldn't be able to lay there for very long, the next sickness spell would soon sweep over me and force me up and back out of the bed.

After being in PICU for about three days, I was still running a fever. Although it was a low-grade fever, it was still a scary factor and everyone was eager to get rid of it. I started having trouble breathing. My heart was beating so fast that I felt as winded as I would if I had just finished sprinting. I didn't understand what was going on with my body. I couldn't eat, I couldn't sleep, and for the past three days, I hadn't gone longer than thirty minutes with out vomiting. I had severe stomach cramps that never went away. At one point, in my delirious state, I remember telling my mom to just let me die. I couldn't live in that kind of pain anymore. I believed in Heaven and God and I was confident that there was a much better place to go to. My physical pain had become so severe that nothing else mattered but finding relief, no matter what the cost.

I asked my doctor at one point why they didn't have a shot or something to give to kids that were terminal and in a lot of pain. She smiled, realizing the kind of pain I was in and what I meant and explained that they couldn't put children down. I wondered why they couldn't; they put dogs down. Then I looked at my mother and realized why. Her entire life is wrapped up in me, as any mother's life is wrapped up in her children. She would never let me go with out a fight, and she definitely wouldn't let anyone put me down. I knew that the idea was absurd, but I couldn't believe that there was nothing anyone could do to ease my pain. Still, they didn't know what was wrong with me, and that was the main problem.

The medical team working on my case had done several tests, and the results were in, but not necessarily clear. Blake came in my room to explain to me that he had read the results and that he wanted to tell me what they meant for my treatment. It turned out that I was positive for c-diff, the same thing that my first nurse in PICU said that I had. My blood cultures also tested positive for three other types of bacteria. I remembered that my brother and dad had told me that a bacteria infection would be the worst; they had been worried that it might be a bacterial infection. Although my brother worked hard to assure me that they didn't think it was anything fatal and that I would be fine, I knew that he was sugar coating the truth. However, I was so sick at that point, I didn't care anymore.

After reviewing my situation, the PICU medical team decided that it would be best to give me time to rest. Since I had been admitted to the PICU, I hadn't slept for longer than two hours at any given time. My vomiting spells kept me awake and the medicine the medical staff was giving me was of no help to my symptoms. The only way my body would be able to rest and rehabilitate would be if they put me on a ventilator and sedated me. My oxygen levels were low which meant that my lungs were having trouble getting enough air. I wondered if I had ARDS again, like the first time I was in PICU, but this time I was taking the next step towards the percentage of ARDS patients that don't survive. Nothing the medical staff gave me helped me sleep or rest. To be honest, when I heard the doctors tell my dad what they wanted to do, I wasn't scared, I was relieved.

"So, I won't be in pain anymore?" I asked hopefully.

"Nope, you'll be asleep, and when you wake up, you'll be better." The doctor explained to me.

"Yes!" I said. Feeling that I could finally see a light at the end of the tunnel.

However, the team wouldn't proceed until they had met with both of my parents. My dad immediately called my family to let them know the situation, so they could rush my mom to the hospital. She had just left the hospital after being with me for almost two days straight to go sleep at the hotel; she had been up for longer than I had. My big brother and sister told Dad they would rush Mom over, while Mom and Dad met with the team, Blake would stay with me in my room and Tab would stay downstairs in the large waiting room with Chandler. Because of health regulations, children under a certain age were not allowed to even enter in the PICU waiting room.

Dad and I sat and waited together in the small glass room for the rest of our family to arrive, we didn't say much to each other. Dad was in deep thought and I was in deep pain. I stared at the double doors that lead into the PICU. It seemed like hours before I finally saw my mom rush through the doors. Her hair was disheveled and her eyes were wild and tired. She was wearing the pajamas she had left in.

I must've stirred or somehow acknowledged her presence in the PICU in some way because my dad turned around, and said, "Oh, Mom's here."

We watched her wash her hands and suit up right outside of my room. She came in and rushed to me, she hugged me and rubbed my arms. She acted as if she never wanted to stop touching me. When she had stayed with me the first time I was in the hospital, I was having freezing spells and she would lay in the bed with me and put her arms around me and hold me. I told her that she couldn't get out of the bed because I needed her body warmth, but it was really the love I felt from her that I liked so much.

"Are Tab and Blake with you?" Dad asked her as she was talking to me and rubbing my head.

"Yeah, they're downstairs with Chandler."

"Alright, well let's go get Blake so that we can go talk to the doctors."

"Will you go get him?" My mom asked, her eyes pleaded with my father.

"Okay." He walked out slowly and consciously, promising to return quickly.

I watched him disappear through the double doors. I looked at my mom, she looked so tired, and she just stared back at me.

"I love you, Mommy." I said to her.

"I love you too, Charlie." She said, with tears in her tired eyes.

My dad returned quickly with Blake as he had promised. Blake came in with a smile on his face, said hello to me, and then immediately started looking over my vitals and studying every machine and bag that was attached to me. Mom and Dad waited for a few moments until the doctor came in to get them. They longingly looked at my brother and I and then left. Blake told me that he would be going back downstairs to take care of Chandler shortly because Tab wanted to come up and see me. I didn't really care, as long as someone in my family was with me. I closed my eyes and dozed off as Blake whispered to himself about all of the machines attached to me and filling up my room.

I woke up to see my sister sitting beside me reading the bible. She was holding my hand with her well sanitized, rubber glove hand. She looked at me and smiled.

"Hey Tab." I said.

"Hey Char."

That's all we said to each other. She sat reading the bible and I sat holding my bucket as we held hands. I closed my eyes and listened to the verses my sister read to me. She skipped around to different books and chapters, but she always came back to Philippians, chapter 4, verse 13. "I can do all things through Christ which strengthens me." She kept going back to it and repeating it. I believed in this verse, and I trusted God with everything I was going through. I was ready to get better; I was ready to go home. I looked at Tab, "Tell Chan I'm sorry." I said gasping for air. She looked at me with her eyes wide and concerned.

"Chandler's not mad at you Charlie, he just doesn't want to have Christmas without you. All of his presents are still sitting, unopened, under the tree. He wants to open them with you, he said he's waiting until you get home."

I smiled, "He'll give in.

I had been watching the clock since my parents left to speak with the doctors. I had asked my mom three days earlier, when I was first put in PICU, when I would be going up to the fourth floor. I thought I would only be in PICU for a little while, but it looked like I may be staying for a lot longer. My parents had been gone for almost an hour and Blake and Tab had been taking turns sitting with me until they returned. I kept watching that clock; I would stare and watch the second hand tick, counting every second that passed. Once I had counted the ticks long enough I would look at the double doors leading into PICU, waiting to see my mom or dad or even one of the doctors on my case.

It had been less than an hour, but it felt like much longer to me, when my parents finally returned with the doctors. My dad explained to me for the second time what the medical staff had decided to do to help my body heal and recover from this sickness I'd been fighting. He explained how the ventilator would breathe for me and give my lungs a much-needed break. I wouldn't wake up until I was better. I wondered for a moment what my chances of actually waking up were.

When I was first diagnosed, I asked my dad to tell me how I would die, if I were to die from leukemia. He explained to me that more than likely it wouldn't actually be the cancer that killed me, it would be a virus or infection I picked up and couldn't fight off because of my weak immune system. He told me that I would probably get really sick, more than likely have a high fever, possibly congestion or nausea. Eventually, I would end up in intensive care. The last step before death would be getting put on a ventilator or biPAP machine. I realized that my experience so far had been almost identical to what my dad had described, but I also realized that other people that were a lot sicker than me survived moments like this all the time. I had explained to my family after my doctors had told us that I would need to have a bone marrow transplant that I didn't want them to tell me anything else as far as survival rates, odds, side-effects, etc. unless I asked. They honored my wishes, and I didn't ask them if they thought I would wake back up.

My medical team wanted to put me on the ventilator immediately. My family came in one by one to tell me they loved me and talk to me one last time before I was put to sleep for an indefinite amount of time. The last person to come see me was my big sister. She kissed and rubbed my head then smiled at me and said, "Well, we'll be right here with you while you're sleeping and we'll be standing right here when you wake up."

"You guys are like Santa Clause!" I said and we both laughed. As we were laughing, the medical team walked in and asked me to roll on my side. They were about to administer the medicine to paralyze me and put me to sleep so they could put me on the ventilator. I looked at my sister as she watched them, I could tell she was scared. I knew that would be a normal emotion to feel, but I wasn't scared, I was relieved to be out of pain. The doctors told my sister that she had to leave. She looked at me and held her fist out.

"Pound it?" I said smiling.

"Yeah." She said smiling back at me. We bumped fist and she said, "I love you, Char."

"I love you too, Tab."

I watched her walk out of the room and stop at the door. She turned around and said, "Remember Philippians four-thirteen!"

"Alright." I smiled and laughed. She lingered, watching me for a moment, and then I watched her as she slowly walked back out to the waiting room, looking back every few seconds to check on me.

The medical team began preparing me for the intubation process where they would stick the tube that was attached to the ventilator down into my lungs. My doctor explained to me that I would be put under deep anesthesia during the intubation, but not for the entire time I was on the ventilator. During the time that I would be on the ventilator, I would be on anesthesia that would keep me unconscious and paralization medication to keep me from fighting against the ventilator. I watched the hospital workers, all women, in different colored scrubs rushing around me in my small glass room. They were pushing buttons and checking stats. They worked around me quickly as I began to doze from the anesthesia they were slowly dripping into my veins.

Tab, Chan, and I at The Wildhorse Saloon

Saying Goodbye

Charlie didn't wake up after the medical staff put him to sleep that day shortly after I walked out of his room. Our family lived in that PICU waiting room for five long, painful days and nights after Charlie was intubated. I never gave up hope that Charlie would wake up out of his coma and beat this horrible disease once and for all. Unfortunately, the Lord needed another angel. And I'll never forget the day the doctors told us that they had done all they could do.

I had excitely left the hospital the night before, happy and hopeful because for the first time, Charlie's stats were up and he seemed to be getting better. I wanted to stay with Charlie, but Chandler needed me with him at home. Since Charlie had been sick, he had clung to me with all his might. I guess having your big sister is the next best thing to having your mom. As I drove him I sung Charlie's favorite song as loud as I could and thanked the Lord for taking care of my little brother. I fell asleep that night holding my other little brother in my arms. His small, seven-year old hands gripped the bracelets I wore to represent Charlie and his foundation. I never took them off.

The next morning, I woke up and hurriedly got ready. I called everyone that was with Charlie to check on how he was doing, everyone assured me that nothing had changed and that I should take my time coming back and get some rest. However, I felt that I needed to get to the hospital as quickly as possible. I felt something rushing me. On the way to the hospital that day, I stopped at our local mall to get Charlie a pair of Michael Jordan high-top basketball shoes. The medical staff wanted to put physical therapy boots on Charlie's feet while he was paralyzed to keep him from losing mobility from lack of circulation. Unfortunately, since Charlie was a two hundred pound, six-foot man in a children's hospital, the medical staff couldn't find any to fit him. I asked the nurse if a pair of high tops would work and she said yes, so I improvised his physical therapy boots, I knew he would love them if he were awake to see them.

I arrived at the hospital sometime in the afternoon and grabbed one of the small red wagons the hospital had littering the parking garage and hallways. I loaded a box of Charlie's LiveLovely t-shirts and bracelets that he had made for his foundation and his Michael Jordan physical therapy boots into the small wagon and ran my way to the elevator and down to the PICU waiting room on the third floor. I couldn't wait to see my little brother.

I walked into that familiar PICU waiting room that I could remember sitting for hours in just a couple months before and praying that my family would never have to come back there, but here we were. As I rolled the little red overflowing wagon into the waiting room full of sullen eyed parents, grandparents, and siblings, praying and waiting to be with the children they loved so much that were so sick on the other side of those double doors. I saw my dad, sitting alone in a small chair next to the door and I walked over to him. I pulled the wagon up beside him and pulled out a shirt for him. He had been wearing the same shirt for days. I also pulled out the shoes I bought for Charlie, Dad smiled but his eyes were sad and worried. He stared at the clock hanging on the wall of the waiting room. Someone in that waiting room always had their eyes on that clock counting down seconds until they were allowed back in to be with their children. As soon as the second hand struck four o'clock PM, my dad and I stood up together and made our way through the double doors. We stopped at the sanitizing station and suited up, as I prepared myself to enter that glass room where my little brother lay sleeping, I stared at him. I still couldn't believe what was happening was real.

Dad and I slid the glass door open and shut it behind us. As we had done every time we walked in to visit Charlie since he was put on the ventilator, we announced who was in the room to see him and what we had been doing since we had been away. We all believed he could hear us, and we had been told by many people including the nurses and doctors that when people are sedated like Charlie, they often report remembering people talking to them when they wake up. My dad and I took turns telling Charlie how wonderful he was and how strong he was and how much we loved him. I took the shoes I had bought them and methodically laced them loosely and tried to slide them on his feet. I had been massaging his feet and working with them since he had been asleep, I didn't want him to wake up and have trouble walking. I couldn't get the shoes I bought him on his feet, they were too small even though I had bought them a size bigger. Charlie's feet were just too swollen.

I looked up and counted over fifteen different IVs hooked up to him, I didn't even know that was possible. I looked at his stats and to my disappointment, they had all began to decline. His oxygen saturation was in the eighties when it should have been in the high nineties. His heart rate was extremely high. His feet were swollen because of poor circulation and he was having trouble getting fluids out of his body on his own so his doctors had started him on dialysis. I kept trying to fit his shoes on his feet, trying to deny that he was too swollen to wear them. Eventually, my dad told me that I had to stop, they weren't going to fit. With tears in my eyes, I shoved the brand new sneakers back into the box and set them on a shelf in Charlie's hospital room. I just stood beside him and held is hand as I watched him lie there, wondering if he knew I was there or if he could feel or hear me.

I was still staring at Charlie and holding his hand when his doctor walked in. She had only been on his case for a few days, and I had not become as comfortable with her as I had been with the other doctors that had worked with Charlie. She was a dark-skinned lady with long dark hair and she spoke with an accent, she spoke to my father using medical jargon. I didn't pay her much attention until I hear her say, "multi organ failure." My heart stopped beating and my blood ran cold through my body. I looked at the doctor with shock and sorrow, I'm sure the color in my face was gone. I looked at my dad to be sure that I had really heard what I thought I heard, he looked back at me and gave me a small nod encouraging me to be strong. "Go call Mom and Blake, they need to get here soon." He said to me. I kissed Charlie on the forehead and walked out to the hallway to call my family in for what was sure to be the hardest experience we would ever have to go through.

When my mother and Blake arrived, we all walked back to be with Charlie together. The doctors told us we didn't have much longer with Charlie. Our extended family were all gathered in the waiting room at this point, many of them had traveled from Kentucky when Charlie was put on the ventilator. As our close-knit family gathered around Charlie, we held him and kissed him and prayed over him. Now that Charlie had taken a turn for the worse, we no longer had to follow the PICU waiting hours, we could stay with him constantly, and we did. For two long days and nights, we fought sleep to be with Charlie every second. We begged God to bring him back, we asked for a miracle. We held on to faith. I remember the only time I fell asleep in that two-day period. Blake and I, along with mom and dad hugged and sang to Charlie for hours. His stats stayed the same and I knew he was fighting to stay with us. Eventually, my brother and I left our parents to be alone with the beautiful angel that we called our little brother. We both believed that Charlie wouldn't be alive when we woke up. We held each other in a quiet, private waiting room the doctors had set aside for situations like ours. We lay on a small, floral print couch in the dark room with the door shut and held each other as we tried to soak in the shock and reality of the death of our little brother. We didn't speak, we knew we were both feeling the same way, we just held each other and cried ourselves to sleep.

We woke up six hours later when a hospital staff worker came in the room and the bright lights of the hospital hallways streamed into our room. The lady told us that we couldn't sleep in the room any longer. I asked her what time it was and she told me that it was ten in the morning. I couldn't believe it, I was sure that we would've been woken up before then to go home. I didn't think Charlie was going to make it that much longer. Blake and I jumped up and put our shoes on, we washed her hands and ran into Charlie's room to see him, suiting up didn't matter anymore, we wanted to touch him skin to skin, not skin to latex. I was delighted to see that his stats had actually improved since the last time I had seen him. He was holding on strong; I kept hoping he would pull through. My dad was sitting in a small chair holding Charlie's hand and my exhausted mother stood on a small stool on Charlie's left side next to his head. She was leaned over the bed with her head on his and singing and kissing him. The nurse told me that she had been doing it all night. When my parents saw we were awake, they let us stay with Charlie alone for a while. They went to the small quiet room to rest for a while, but we all knew that there wasn't any real rest in that hospital.

I took over Mom's position of singing and rubbing my head against his. Blake took over Dad's position and sat and held his hand. We had been in there for about an hour and I hadn't stopped singing to Charlie. We had figured out that music seemed to always help Charlie's stats. A few days earlier, when we still had to obey the visiting hours, we put his iPod on his favorite playlist to listen to until we came back. When we walked back in two hours later, his stats looked great. We started putting his iPod on every time we left his room. Now, we just sang his favorite songs over and over again. Through out the day we all took turns going in and holding Charlie's hand and rubbing his head and singing. At one point the doctor came in to look at Charlie's eyes. My brother had explained to me that they watched the pupils reactions to the light to see if there was brain activity. Before I had gone to sleep the night before, the doctor said his pupils were not reacting to the light. The next day, December 31st, 2008, she raised his eyelids and shined her light in each of his eyes. Her look of surprise and shock said it all, his pupils were responding. This gave us tremendous joy and we continued singing and praying and holding Charlie. Everyone took turns spending time with him; the usual people were constantly in and out Blake, Mom, Dad, Uncle Perry, Aunt Barbara, and myself. Our Mamaw and our other aunts and uncles, as well as cousins all came to support Charlie and visit with him.

At one moment, our entire family sat in a large circle in the middle of the tiny PICU waiting room. We all wore our LiveLovely bracelets and t-shirts in show of our support for Charlie, as we sat, we were joined by the oncology nurses that had come to be known as "Charlie's Angels," Angela, Catherine, and Leslie. Our hearts were heavy and our minds worried, and my dad took the moment to say a prayer that would forever touch the hearts of everyone else sitting in the waiting room. I watched my forty-two year old father's eyes fill with tears as he spoke, "Let's all get on our knees and say this one prayer for Charlie together." Our whole family, including myself and all three of Charlie's Angels got up out of our seats and kneeled in our circle holding hands with our heads down. My father raised his head to the sky, talking directly to the Lord, "God, we come to you in a time of need. We had this same prayer sixteen weeks into our pregnancy with Charlie. We thought we had lost him then. Lord we ask you to put your hands on Charlie and do your will. We pray you to take care of him Lord and if it be in your will, Lord, please, let us keep him again." We all cried and said "Amen" in unison together.

At about eleven o'clock that evening, my mom sat in the waiting room with Blake and I. My dad took all of our relatives that had made it there back to visit with Charlie. Dad had just walked back with the last visitors, his mother, our Mamaw Faye, and his oldest sister, our Aunt Linda, when Mom leaned up in her seat and stared Blake and I both in the eye. "We need to get back there." She said. "It's time." That's all she said, and the three of us got up together and walked through the double doors of the PICU and back to Charlie's little glass room. Blake began to sob before we entered the room and told us that he would come back just before midnight so that we could all count down the New Year with Charlie. He left and so did the other visitors, including my dad. My mother and I stood on stools on either side of Charlie's bed. He was so big. I remembered when his tiny baby hand was just a third of the size of my tiny six-year-old hand. Now, even though he wasn't finished growing, his hand was twice the size of mine and he was a half-foot taller than me. He barely fit in the little bed he was in. The bed was raised up, to help Charlie breathe better, so he was almost sitting upright. Mom held his right side as I held his left side and we sang his favorite song over and over. We no longer wore masks or gloves; we just kissed him and touched him flesh to flesh. I could feel his love wash over us as my mother and I, the two women in his life, held him tight and rubbed him gently. I looked up at the round, black, analog clock that hung on the wall above my head, there were only ten minutes left until the New Year.

"Okay, Charlie." I began. "There are only ten minutes left until the New Year. Blake and Dad will be in here to spend it with us, and you're going to be my New Year's kiss, okay? I'm going to be the luckiest girl in the world." Tears welled up in my eyes as I spoke. I wished he could answer back and make a joke out of all of this; he was the only person that ever knew how to make me laugh when I felt like my world had crashed around me. I wished that he could be out with his friends at a high school party, at Julianna or Ju Ju's house, Charlie's best girl friend. He had spent the last few New Years there and I was sure that all the girls probably hoped that they would be Charlie's kiss, this year he was all mine, although bittersweet, I felt lucky.

Dad and Blake walked into the small glass room to be with us at exactly five minutes until midnight. Dad announced to Charlie that we were all together in his room with him and that we were going to spend these last few minutes of this year all together. We surrounded Charlie, hugging and kissing him. We kept checking the analog clock hanging on the wall, the clock that Charlie had watched for so many days waiting for the minute he would finally get to leave that glass room, every minute that passed we would announce to Charlie that we were that much closer to the new year. As the new year quickly approached, we all huddled together, holding onto what time we had left together. We all stared at the clock about to announce to Charlie that there was only one minute left until the new year. When the second hand struck the 12 on the clock at exactly 11:59 PM December 31, 2008, we all witnessed what was to me, a miracle. The presence in the room was overwhelming; we could feel love and joy pouring out all over our family, all over Charlie. The second hand stopped, abruptly on that twelve and my family and I listened to the internal struggle that the clock was having. It sounded as if the clock wanted to continue on ticking, continue counting the time, but something was holding, something was trying to stop the time. We were all shocked and amazed at what we were witnessing, we knew that this was no coincidence, but we also knew that we only had seconds before the new year was upon us and we had to celebrate it with Charlie, we all knew it would be his last one.

Our dad hurried out the sliding glass door checking for the other clocks, they were all still working, only Charlie's had stopped. Dad begged someone to give him the time and a nurse sitting at the nurse's stations shouted, "I have ten seconds!" We all surrounded Charlie's bed, me on his right side, Mom on his left and Dad and Blake standing at his feet. We counted down together, all of us choking back tears, "Ten, nine, eight, seven, six, five, four, three, two, one, Happy New Year, Charlie!" I kissed him directly on his lips, sweetly and softly. It was the most precious kiss of my life. After I kissed him and held him close, I moved to the foot of his bed and laid my hand on him to let everyone else get their kisses in. After everyone had personally wished Charlie a Happy New Year, Dad decided that we should all tell Charlie that we loved him at the same time. Again, in unison, choking back tears, we shouted, "Three, two, one, we love you, Charlie!" At the moment the second hand on the clock was released and I heard the loudest tick of time that I had ever heard. Again, my family looked in amazement at the clock. As everyone else stared at the clock, I looked at Charlie and smiled, I knew that this was his way of letting us know that life goes on and that we were going to be okay. At that very moment, upon the clock's release, I was blessed to feel the most powerful feeling of joy and love I had ever felt. It rushed through me like electricity; I must have made a sound when I felt this euphoric feeling because my entire family was looking at me. I felt as if my feet were no longer touching the floor. It was like Charlie had gone right through me or like he had picked me up and held me; I could never give justice to that moment in that hospital room with simple words. I know, with every ounce of my soul, that that moment was the closest I will get to Heaven until the day I die. My family could see in my eyes the revelation I had experienced and there was no need for them to ask questions. They parted from next to Charlie as I rushed to his side, shaking all over; I held his head in my hands and kissed the bare flesh where there had once been hair. My tears splashed on him and I wiped them off, I knew that he was gone. I just knew. I knew that what was left was his body, it was clear that Charlie's spirit had left that room and left this earth. I cried, because even though his heart was still beating, I knew he was gone.

For the next hour and forty minutes, the four of us, Mom, Dad, Blake, and myself stayed with Charlie. Mom laid her head on top of his as she stood on a stool on his left side and Dad stood behind her, holding his left hand. Blake laid his head on Charlie's chest and just listened to his heartbeat. I laid my head on Blake's back and held Charlie's right hand. I looked up at the screen that showed in different, bright colors, all of Charlie's vitals. His oxygen saturation was dropping quickly, from eighty-six that morning down, to seventy-six now and still declining. I focused on his heartbeat, for almost an entire week now, his heart had been racing at the same speed that a person's heart rate would be if they were sprinting. At its highest it was about one hundred and eighty-six beats per minute. I watched it decline to sixty and then bounce back up, and it declined even further and bounced back up to about one-hundred, then it quickly declined to twenty, to ten, and then to zero. I though my heart would stop too when I saw that zero, I prayed as hard as I could, begging God to make it change again, to make it bounce back as it had been doing, but it stayed there. The ventilator was still hooked up to Charlie, so it sounded as if he were still breathing, but we all knew the bitter truth as we looked at each other with weary, cried out eyes. The nurse came in and turned off the monitor that displayed Charlie's vitals, then the doctor came in and put her stethoscope on his chest, she just nodded her head and pronounced him at exactly 1:40 AM on January 1, 2009. Although the pain of having to say good-bye to him so early has never gone away, and I know it probably never will, I hold on to the promise I was given and the faith that I hold from that small little clock in that glass hospital room where my wise little brother closed his eyes for the last time.

As I sit here today, writing this story, to share with the world, I realized that some people might not believe some of the things I've written. Some people may not believe in the clock like I do, but they weren't there in that moment, and I can tell you with out a doubt that what happened was real. Because of it, my faith in a life after this one is stronger than ever. The one person in my life that tried to show me faith was my little brother. I told him that if he died, I wouldn't want to live anymore. I told him that I wouldn't know what to do without him. I hated life and if God did exist, I hated him too for allowing Charlie to have cancer. Charlie responded to me with this quote, I hope you find as much hope and peace in the words of this wise young man as I have, "We can't see everything in the full picture it was meant to be seen in now. So many people view experiences in life and the path that we travel on as a series of coincidences. They cannot see the full picture. They believe that they see the full picture, but in reality, they are simply seeing one small part; one tiny picture inside of a collage of billions of pictures that together create one magnificent, pure portrait. Every thing that happens, big or small will have an impact on at least one person. If that one person has family or friends, then it will also affect their family and friends. If those friends of family or friends of friends have family and friends then it will also affect them. In some way, everyone will be touched. It's the individual that must decide what they will do with their experience, and if it will make them better and stronger or tear them down.

Death brings with it the most suffering for the people who are left behind. It is a beautiful part of life for the person that experiences it, and each person, in their own time, will realize the beauty of death as they realize the beauty of life, the two go hand in hand."

The LIVE LOVELY
Foundation

"I CAN DO ALL THINGS
THROUGH CHRIST WHICH STRENGTHENS ME."

- PHILIPPIANS 4:13

LIVELOVELY'S MISSION IS TO PROMOTE
AWARENESS OF THE ADOLESCENT AND
YOUNG ADULT (AYA) CANCER SURVIVAL GAP
AND TO RAISE FUNDS FOR RESEARCH,
HOSPITALS, AND INDIVIDUAL FAMILIES THAT
ARE AFFECTED BY THE AYA CANCER SURVIVAL GAP.

TO JOIN US IN OUR MISSION,
OR TO LEARN MORE VISIT
LIVELOVELY.ORG